DOORKEEPERS OF

REVIVAL

BIRTHING, BUILDING, AND SUSTAINING REVIVAL

KIM OWENS

DESTINY IMAGE® PUBLISHERS, INC.
P.O. Box 310, Shippensburg, PA 17257-0310
"Promoting Inspired Lives."

This book and all other Destiny Image and Destiny Image Fiction books are available at Christian bookstores and distributors worldwide.

For more information on foreign distributors, call 717-532-3040.
Reach us on the Internet: www.destinyimage.com.

ISBN 13 TP: 978-0-7684-6149-7
ISBN 13 eBook: 978-0-7684-6150-3
ISBN 13 HC: 978-0-7684-6152-7
ISBN 13 LP: 978-0-7684-6151-0

For Worldwide Distribution, Printed in the U.S.A.
1 2 3 4 5 6 7 8 / 25 24 23 22 21

Contents

Preface

Our story is important to your success in birthing, building, and sustaining revival. In this book, I will share our personal revival journey along with crucial spiritual components and revelatory deposits to help you develop revival in your life and church. I have included key parts of our journey that are what I call "threshold moments." A threshold is a crossing over from what is, to what is to be. To successfully host sustained revival, you must be willing to learn to recognize and crossover those crucial threshold moments. They will be frequent but each crossing over brings a greater spiritual capacity for revival, which brings greater tenacity to sustain a move of God in your life and church.

Note from the Publisher

Doorkeepers of Revival is one of the great revival books of our day. Long before any discussions of working with Pastor Kim Owens on this project, I was recommending her book left and right, as I am convinced that the language contained in these pages is going to call the body of Christ into a substantial *upgrade*. Don't let that word *upgrade* scare you. We are being *upgraded* back into normal. Upgraded into the Acts Chapter 2 Bible blueprint that paints a picture of what "normal Christianity" should look like. Read this book with an expectation that your heart will *burn for revival,* page after page, line upon line. Why? Kim Owens has never graduated from being hungry for more of God. And it's voices like hers that we need so desperately in this hour to boldly remind us: "Church, *there is so much MORE!*" This is why it is with great excitement that I recommend this book to you. Truly, books like *Doorkeepers of Revival* are what Destiny Image was founded to distribute to the world!

Larry Sparks
Publisher, *Destiny Image*
(May 2021)

Foreword

I was privileged to be the senior pastor at Brownsville
Assembly of God in Pensacola, Florida, during the
revival that lasted five years from 1995-2000. There is
nothing like revival! It is spontaneous, life changing, and
God sent. Revival must be prepared for, prayed in, and
protected with compassionate and delicate hands.

In her new book, Doorkeepers of Revival, Kim Owens
has emerged as a voice that must be heard. Although revival
is powerful and resilient, it must be stewarded. We are living
in such a precarious period of time in many ways. Just about
everywhere I go, I hear from Christian leaders that are deeply
concerned regarding false teachings and heresies that have
slipped into ministries and have taken root. The atmosphere
of revival seems to be such an environment that affects a
myriad of silly notions that masquerade as sound doctrine.

I was raised under a spiritual father and mentor. One
thing he always told me was to never try to answer questions
that people are not asking. Today, with all that is going on in

the world, people are asking many questions. Kim Owens provides answers to many of these questions concerning revival in Doorkeepers of Revival.

This book will serve as a modern-day epistle to those in revival and those seeking it. Kim is a doorkeeper. She does not just know about revival but has experienced it firsthand. She is a modern-day Deborah who is strong and committed without apology. As a doorkeeper, Kim talks about things that would be difficult to read about elsewhere.

Spiritual hunger and curiosity abound today and represent significant opportunities for the Church to step up and take our place in this last day move of God. The question is, will the Church be ready, or will it resort to the counterfeit to try and satisfy this hunger?

Doorkeepers of Revival stirs my soul. These pages will serve as a spiritual transfusion to those who feel weak and anemic in their walk with God. Thank you, Kim, for such a word. I can see that God is raising you up, not just as an echo, but as a voice!

John Kilpatrick
Senior pastor of Church of His Presence
Pastor of The Brownsville Revival

Introduction
Doorkeepers of Revival

*U*pon our arrival in 1997 as new lead pastors of our church here in Phoenix, Arizona, we found a congregation that was ready for change and a move of the Holy Spirit. This was both encouraging and challenging all at the same time as this was our very first senior pastorate. Working in our favor was the already instilled revival culture and atmosphere. While there was not a full-blown outpouring happening at that moment, the church had received years of impartation of a revival spirit and it was already in the DNA of the people. One of the primary reasons we were called to assume the pastorate of this church was to *"keep the revival spirit alive"* or you could say be the *"doorkeepers of revival."* The founding pastors had been revivalists themselves and because of our previous friendship and their familiarity with my husband's family and his ministry mantle, they felt strongly that we should be asked to come and continue to steward this revival atmosphere.

We began with this agenda but met great resistance as our journey unfolded. Every imaginable type of warfare came against us. Demonic, physical, emotional, mental, spiritual and relational attacks seemed relentless for a long season. As a result of the resistance and not knowing at the time how to properly deal with it in the spirit realm, we found ourselves in a season of barrenness and headed away from our original assignment as *doorkeepers of revival.* There is one thing you must know as you contend for revival: *Revival is war!* I will develop this thought more later in the book. At this juncture, please know that your level of desire and hunger for revival will be met with that exact level of demonic resistance and warfare. You must have *a revival resolve.* You must commit to being a *doorkeeper of revival.*

Before I unfold the rest of our story, let's begin with a definition of revival. We like to say that it is: *the sustained presence and power of God that results in transformation.* While there have been many definitions of revival, for the purpose of this book, we will look at revival through the lens of *longevity, sustainability and permanence.* It is never meant for us to digress from the point of revival. It seems to be a current belief that revival can come but will inevitably die out. A revival shouldn't be defined by only a three to five-year "*run*"; it should be fought for every moment of our lives and in our ministries.

While I realize that there are ebbs and flows of *how* the Spirit moves, and that we cannot dictate when or where He shows up, I don't believe we have to sacrifice powerful moves of the Spirit because we're not doing what it takes to *keep the fire burning and the door open to revival.* Never forget that revival requires an open door, an access, or an entry point. This entry point is the place of personal and corporate hunger and pursuit of more of God in prayer and personal sacrifice. The element of "demand" is forever a part of sustained revival. We must be willing to consistently place a demand for more of God and allow Him to make a demand on the intensity of our spiritual pursuit.

So, here is the bottom line to sustaining revival: doing what it takes, no matter how long it takes, to keep *the door of revival* open and the *fire burning on the altar.* Sustained revival is not only what the Lord desires, but I believe it is what most Christians and pastors desire and it is what the world needs to see: a church ablaze with Holy Ghost fire. But an all-important question remains, are we willing to do what it takes?

This book will hopefully spark a flame and give you a glimpse into the depth of hunger, spiritual pursuit, spiritual resolve and focus that it takes to sustain revival, specifically in the local church but also in our personal lives. I am writing this for all the hungry hearts of pastors, ministry leaders and Christians who have searched for more but have had to settle for the status quo thinking that what we have is all there is and it's just *the "way" things are done now.*

You may have heard it said or implied that revival is old school, outdated, and no one wants to be defined by it any longer. I have good news; revival isn't outdated and there are scores of hungry hearts that are seeking for more of Holy Spirit in their churches and lives. New techniques and ideals may have sidelined revival, but it's the way Jesus started His Church and is the way He will culminate it. The Acts Church began in revival and the book of Revelation shows us that Jesus will come back for a Church in revival, a Church that walks in purity, authority and uninhibited passion for Him. He made it clear that He's not returning for a lukewarm, passive, distracted or carnal people, He's returning for a passionate, warring Bride!

It is my sincere hope that our personal journey in revival will set your heart ablaze with the fire of Pentecost and ignite within you a fervent hunger to keep the fire burning on the altar, and become *a doorkeeper of revival!*

Chapter One
Doorkeeper Defined

A doorkeeper allows access and entry. A doorkeeper has keys. A doorkeeper has authority. A doorkeeper is a watchman, protector, and guardian of the entry point. They occupy a position and an assignment and at all costs will *not allow the door to go unattended.*

In the assignment of sustained revival, a doorkeeper guards the door making certain that *revival* has an access point. If there is no entry point, revival will not come. There is a constant, and I stress a constant *watch* at the door making sure that it's open to revival. While this book will cover many areas to which must be watched over, know for now that the decision to be a doorkeeper of revival is not one that cannot be taken lightly. This is not just another *method* for the church; *it is the mantle* for the Church. Methods for doing church can come and go, and we can take or leave them, but a mantle demands accountability and must be worn, embraced, and stewarded. Once we have the revelation that *revival is a mantle* passed along to us by the Early Church we will understand that it is not negotiable, redefinable, nor refusable. The privilege to host His presence and allow Him to move anyway He desires in the lives of people and the context of our churches is *holy* and it is to be cherished and championed.

> The privilege to host His presence and allow Him to move anyway He desires in the lives of people and the context of our churches is holy and it is to be cherished and championed.

Jacob Became a Doorkeeper

Jacob encountered God at a place he named Bethel. That day, *Bethel became the access point for revival.* God used *this location* to enter Jacob's world. When God enters our realm and world, His agenda is to always establish His purposes. He accomplishes this through you and me and many times if not most, everything changes. Names change, addresses change, mindsets change and attitudes change. Bethel is an access point for the impartation of His realm. Bethel is the place of encounter, the place where heaven opens and God is revealed. When you've experienced Bethel, you'll know it. Neither you nor anyone else will be able to deny that God has come and *revival has entered the door.*

The Bible says that Jacob dreamt that angels were ascending to heaven and descending to earth. When he awoke from his sleep, however, he declared, "Surely the Lord is in this place…how awesome is this place, this is none other than the house of God and this is the gate of heaven." (Genesis 28:16-17). God's house is where God's presence dwells and like Jacob, we're to erect a perpetual pillar to His presence, or we could say, a sustained focus to keep the door open for continual, free access and entry of God into our realm, our world.

If we're going to be a doorkeeper of revival, we must first commit to being His House. His House requires that we prioritize His presence above everything else. Hence, it must be our identifying mark and trait and it must drive everything else. His presence must be the center of it all because *His presence is revival.* We must concede that His presence defines His House. We've tried too long to do it without Him, it's time to come back to Bethel and take our position at the door of heaven and allow Him access to our realm, our world. Then when the world walks into our church or encounters our lives they will have no option but to say, "surely the Lord is in this place," "this is the House of God" and "a gate of heaven." When we become His House, a place that prioritizes His presence, we are then a door for His realm, an access point for heaven, and we are truly *doorkeepers of revival.*

Finding Your Peniel

Jacob had another encounter with God at a place he named Peniel. Peniel means "face of God." It was there Jacob wrestled and contended for "more." His heart cry was, *do not release me, Lord, until I have more of You, until I see revival!* Jacob received the answer to his cry, *h*e encountered the Face of God. When you encounter someone's face, you're looking into the most revealing part of their physical being; you see their essence, attitude, and intentions. You are *personal* with them because you're in their *space.* Revival is getting into God's face and space. It is an encounter with His essence, attitude, and intentions. It is intimate and personal, and you never leave the same. You leave *every* encounter with a limp, a new understanding of your identity, and a touch of heaven in your heart. You have become an access point for revival.

The place of encounter has been lost in many of our modern church settings. Corporately, the altars have literally been replaced with more seats and spiritually less time is available to tarry. Personally, the altars have been replaced with competing secular weights and sins that fill our schedules and minds. The byproduct is empty hearts that lack zeal, shallow relationships with Jesus, and a lack of the fire of the Holy Ghost in our atmospheres. We cannot expect to have revival if the place of encounter is replaced. Revival requires encounter and encounter requires intentional time, effort, and the priority on finding His space and encountering His face.

In this book, you'll learn about revival that is sustained, but the key element will be your consecration to keeping the door open, no matter how long, no matter the sacrifice. You'll have to continually pray your way into His space where you're forever changed and altered by His glory DNA. You'll have to find Bethel, Peniel and your own altar where you're marked by God and by Him alone. It may require an identity change, lifestyle changes, and church structural changes as you consistently encounter spiritual thresholds that demand more sacrifice of flesh and more wrestling in the spirit.

When you reach this point, you have become His House, you're now a gate, an entry point...a *doorkeeper for revival.*

Chapter Two
Marked by God

*D*uring a daily Bible reading in 1 Kings, something stood out to me about the distinguishing mark of the presence of God. "Hear in heaven, Your dwelling place, and do according to all that the stranger asks of You, *so that all peoples of the earth may know Your name [and Your revelation of Your presence] and fear and revere You,* as do Your people Israel, and may know *and* comprehend that this house which I have built is called by Your Name [and *contains the token of Your presence*]." (1 Kings 8:43 AMPC)

A "token" can be defined as a characteristic or a *MARK* of something. It struck my attention that, as Solomon prayed, he specifically asked the Lord that just as Israel (type of the Church) had revelation of His presence, the world would have revelation of His presence and that they would know that the Temple was distinguished or *"marked by" His presence.*

The Mark of His Presence

I want to be "marked by His Presence" and I want His Church to be marked by His Presence. I have observed that so many ministers and churches are allowing other things to mark them. They're known for successful efforts in so many things but intentionally hosting His presence isn't one of them. Because of this, I wonder if many have lost the revelation of the necessity of His authentic presence.

Having grown up in the Church and now as an ordained minister in the Church, I have seen the ebbs and flows of the Body of Christ and the five-fold ministry and how we have a tendency to stray from our *primary purpose to be marked and permeated with the presence of the Lord.* We have a tendency to replace it with shallow substitutes motivated by selfish ambitions that bring attention to us rather than Him and fuel our egos rather than

> When you take the tangible presence of God away from the Church you become just like any other gathering of people.

God's heart. When you take the tangible presence of God away from the Church you become just like any other gathering of people.

May we never forget that it is ONLY His presence that separates us from others. Moses said it like this: "If Your presence does not go with us, do not bring us up from here…is it not in Your going with us that we are distinguished, I and your people, from all the other people upon the face of the earth?" (Exodus 33:15-16) What else is going to distinguish us or mark us from any other group of people who gather for things such as a ball game, party, club or backyard BBQ? All of these are gathering or assemblies of people. It's only His presence that marks His Church. When we remove the emphasis from His manifested presence, we have nothing of substance to offer the world. When Isaiah saw a vision of the Lord filling the Temple, he saw the train of the Lord, or the substance of the Lord permeating the place. *This measure of presence will be the only thing that can truly penetrate the dense darkness of the hearts of people and the only thing that truly satisfies a hungry heart.* My concern is that we are busier

> When we remove the emphasis from His manifested presence, we have nothing of substance to offer the world.

planning our series of sermons, how to market them, and what entertainment will accompany them to keep the attention of the hearers rather than paying the price in the Secret Place to get His presence to *mark us and change us.*

I am convinced that if we will pay the price, He will MARK us, and the enticement for people to attend will not be the latest graphic technique or culturally relevant word or phrases. It will be because God's presence permeates me and the atmosphere of my church. Then when people come, they see and experience Him! When they experience Jesus, everything changes and they will change everything around them because of His presence.

After 36 years in the ministry, I'm at a season where real and authentic is very important to me and it takes a lot to impress me. Titles, positions, degrees, travel itineraries, names and notoriety are less important than the real mark of the presence of God on a life or ministry. If they've got *"the MARK"*, then I'm thankful because I know they paid a very high price for it.

Marking Not Marketing

We are at a crucial crossroads in the Church. We've had a decade or more where we have tried to redefine ourselves without the manifest presence of God. God has no room or time to mark us because we're so busy marketing ourselves and even worse, we're believing our own press. The Bible warns against comparing ourselves by ourselves and this has been the culture of the church for too long. We've become a generation obsessed with numbers, financial success and social media "likes". We have forgotten that it is the Holy Spirit and His Word who should be setting our standards, not our peers.

We've confused anointing with talent, exchanged commotion for devotion and substituted a good time for the Glory. We've exalted corporation above consecration and convenience above conviction. It's time to get His mark back on His Church! In a revival culture, *the mark* must be His presence. There are so many other popular positions that can mark you, but they leave a spiritual deficit that rings hollow and a spiritual atmosphere that is void of substance. This cannot be an option for a doorkeeper of revival. Our constant desire is unrestrained pursuit of the presence of God, we won't settle for anything less.

We currently have a lot of branding and marketing by human ingenuity, but what we desperately need is the branding of the fire of God that *leaves a MARK so indelible that it's undeniable.* God wants to kindle a *burning* in His Church in this hour that makes us firebrands. A branding by fire was the trademark of the early believers. They were accused of being drunk, and a host of other slanders, but no one could deny the fiery mark of God's presence that had been burned into them in the Upper Room encounter. People perceived they had been with Jesus. The religious admitted that if God was behind this early Church that nothing could stop it and they were right because nothing did. It continues and we are them. They were doorkeepers of revival and so are we. This mark of His presence comes with a price and much of it is the pressure of being seared with Him in secret in order to have an imprint of Him in public. May we no longer use our ministries and anointing to impress but make it a priority to get His impression on us. Marked by God!

Marked Ones are Firebrands

Branding is defined as "a mark made by burning." God wants to ignite a burning in you, so you'll become a firebrand through which others can be marked by His glory. A firebrand is one who ignites, stirs, motivates and provokes. May we be used to provoke others to a burning for Him that marks them forever.

I am more hopeful today as I see the tide turning and revival desire rising in the hearts of the remnant church. The shallow substitutes are running their course and Christians are weary from running on empty and merely sitting week after week in their churches' empty atmospheres. Things are coming full circle. God always has a way of bringing us back to Him and Him alone. In a world that is marked by evil and chaos, may the righteous revival remnant arise and choose to be *marked by God*.

Our story is a journey into revival where we desired no other branding or mark than His presence. Our goal was for people to be able to say when they left our services that, "the Presence of God was powerful in that place today!" And because of this, everything we do revolves around that alone: *the move of God is our priority*, the manifestation of His presence

> The motivation of every church service is to be marked by God!

pushes other non-essentials to the back burner and the motivation of every church service is to be *marked by God*.

Chapter Three
Our Revival Story: The Journey

*W*e became frustrated as leaders of our church about eight years or so into our journey. In 2005 my husband was involved in a serious motorcycle accident that resulted in the amputation of his lower left leg. While that story could probably be a book, the bottom line is, this is where the significant warfare against revival began. While the accident itself was *evidence* of the warfare, the impact of the spiritual battle related to the accident wasn't fully understood for many years.

Present Pain is About Future Purpose

My husband, as well as our daughter and I, navigated several years of personal adjustment while also attempting to facilitate a revival mantle of which we did not yet realize the value of or the potential. What we couldn't see then was that *our pain of the moment was leading us to an authority of a mantle.* Never forget, *your present pain is always about your future purpose.* It's not about the moment it's about the momentum that God wants to launch you into.

It took almost a decade for us to make the full turn into revival. By 2013, all of these unrelenting attacks set us back physically, emotionally and especially corporately in our church body. The enemy's warfare against revival is *strategic.* He recognizes mantles of grace more than we so he will formulate a battle strategy to take you out before you arrive.

> The enemy's warfare against revival is *strategic.* He recognizes mantles of grace more than we so he will formulate a battle strategy to take you out before you arrive.

The spirits of Jezebel (an intimidating, manipulating spirit that's after your spiritual authority), and Korah (the uprising of people that believe they know more than you and want to usurp your authority). As well as an Absalom spirit (sent to divide in order to build Satan's own kingdom), a Python spirit (sent to restrict and constrict in all areas, especially prayer and the prophetic). Last, but certainly not least, a religious spirit (an anti-freedom, settling spirit, acceptance of the status quo) were consistently arising in our corporate midst to bring a push back and resistance to the release of revival.

Many times it would take us long periods to recoup personally and corporately from these attacks. All of these attacks are launched to wear you down and make you quit. During those years we repeatedly faced them all. What we realize now is that every battle was training us to wear a mantle of revival that would host His presence, take territory, touch nations and *train doorkeepers of revival.*

Never Settle

Before arriving at that point, however, we had reached a very low place in our resolve. Many times, it is at the point of desperation that revival is released. Our defenses are down and we come to the end of ourselves, we finally realize that we're desperate for God to intervene. Unfortunately, our thought processes as spiritual leaders often become tainted to settle for anything that will bring a significant crowd and give the appearance of success whether it has a move of God on it or not. You don't need to be a revivalist to make this happen, just a good CEO. This takes low-level spiritual sacrifice and usually brings more glory to us than God. So, desperation, depletion and digression are, unfortunately, how God must get our attention to make us choose Him and the move of His spirit above all the other things that bid for our attention to achieve success.

The manifestation of His sustained presence that continually results in transformation is undeniably the only way that Jesus wants to build His Church. My prayer is that *I can make you hungry to push aside the models of a successful church and run for the mantle…of revival.*

> My prayer is that I can make you hungry to push aside the models of a successful church and run for the mantle...of revival.

Some of the battles that we walked through were of significant proportion and some minor but all affect you as a spiritual leader more deeply than you realize. The enemy wants to beat you down and, unfortunately, we didn't understand the magnitude of the spiritual warfare in that season. We knew enough to know it was the devil, yet not enough to know how to rise above it victoriously and consistently.

As I stated earlier, it's very important that you understand the type of warfare against a revival culture. The enemy doesn't want you to press into the fullness of the Spirit, because the more you press, the more of the tangible presence of heaven you release on earth and the more territory you take. If he can keep you *nominal* in your spiritual pursuit and corporate pursuit then he knows he will keep you *natural*. But if we ever get a taste of more, he knows it will lead us out of natural into the supernatural.

Big Church or Big Revival?

In the modern church era we have created a man-focused, entertainment-based, humanistic "pop" Church culture that is far from presence-driven. There may be good music with very talented musicians and even a nice, palatable, encouraging word or "talk" given by a charismatic communicator. However, the substance and tangibility of His realm, presence and glory are missing.

The modern church has evolved into how big we can become in name, numbers and notoriety rather than how big our hearts are in sacrifice zeal and passion for God. While I am not opposed to big churches and believe that God wants to build and bless big churches, He also wants a *big move of His Holy Spirit in those big churches.* We must never forget that before 3000 was added to the Acts Church they had a full-on Holy Ghost encounter in the Upper Room.

Heaven opened over those people. They found Bethel. They found Peniel. They found revival. They became doorkeepers in that Upper Room. Everything that happened after that was a result of their spiritual encounter when suddenly a sound came, a wind came, and the fire came and that was when revival came. Jesus sent them UP (to the Upper Room) before He sent them OUT. They became doorkeepers before they became soul winners. Afterward, everything they touched had the imprint of revival on it and the result was a world turned upside for the Kingdom of God.

Mission Statement Vexation

When we came to our church in 1997, it was the peak of the "build a vision and mission statement" philosophy. The theory was: If you keep saying this vision and mission over and over to the people, they will buy into it and then your church will grow. Everywhere you went that's all you heard.

While we believed in both vision and mission and making a statement of it, we also found that it alone was empty.

Just working a mission statement without the Spirit behind it was draining and unfulfilling to us. Called to be revivalists, we found that the confines of just a paragraph that contained a statement was severely limiting to what was in our spirits. These strategies seemed hollow at best and frustrating at worst. However, as young pastors we had an ambition to be successful in our own eyes and others. So, we were naïve enough to try anything that came down the pike to make that perceived success happen, even if it compromised the mantle of revival.

We began to see some numerical growth for about the first five years or so, but then things began to shift in the spiritual atmosphere over our city. The ease with which we engaged the Spirit in our services became more arduous and, at that time, we didn't understand what was happening in the spirit realm. We looked to the natural more than the spiritual as the culprit. We continued to have a level of His presence, as well as altar calls for salvation and spiritual encounter.

As time went on, however, we were digressing from the spiritual *press* that it takes to release and sustain a revival culture. This was not intentional, but because of the demonic resistance, the personal ambition and the added trendy pressure of "*this* is how you grow a church now," we began to turn away from the most crucial elements that release and sustain revival; passionate prayer, intentional altars, uninhibited truth in preaching and building a spiritual people.

All of this was fueling our frustration in which we found ourselves just prior to the outbreak of revival. It brought us to the place where we had to decide if we were going to build this thing from a mission statement and a few good man-made ideas or were we going to pay the price to go all out for glory, revival, Holy Spirit, and transformational altar encounters? We had to wrestle with the fact that the only way we would be truly fulfilled was to go with the latter. To go with the first required good organizational skills and a corporate mindset, the latter required a complete death to self and any desire for a personal reputation. We knew we could go one route and possibly increase the church size but we could never forget that we were brought here to be *doorkeepers of revival*. We knew that anything less wasn't our assignment and we had to get real honest and commit to who and what God had mantled us to be.

What IS the Definition of "Church"?

Every believer, church, pastor and spiritual leader goes through seasons of definition and discovery of their assignment. However, the attacks we experienced were more than personal, it was an assassination attempt of the enemy to *silence a revival sound that would literally impact nations.* These attacks brought a personal and corporate unsettledness that resulted in a struggle with identity. Therefore, we must keep a strong resolve to stay true to what God has mantled us to be in birthing, building and sustaining a revival culture.

Unsettledness and lack of resolve bring an uncertainty of the call. So be very aware that if you're frequently changing your culture, trying to share revival culture with another, or have any doubts at all, it can bring an identity crisis that stifles revival. But when you embrace the mantle and establish it, everyone is secure knowing and having found identity and that it literally frightens the enemy. The devil is fearful of the one who knows their mantle, identity and assignment. God cannot fully release you into your destiny until you have settled all of these issues. This is why we mustn't be swayed by concepts that lead us away from revival culture. Be confident of this one thing: when you host His presence, everything changes for the good. It may not always be comfortable, but it will always be spiritually profitable.

While we can learn from the values and insight from certain circles and camps of the Body of Christ, we came to understand that The Church was really becoming more of a corporation than it was about camp meeting. the moving of the Spirit and an encounter with God. The praise and worship had become a performance and the shout of the Church was hollow, the prayer meeting empty and its spiritual authority low because the Spirit was not being pursued.

Yes, there was a Church, but there was no Bethel, no Peniel, no entry point for heaven and our hearts were becoming very hungry for the open heaven at Bethel, the face of God at Peniel and the fire found in that Upper Room. We came to the place that if this is all there is to church then we really didn't want to do it.

This Day We Fight!

So, in 2013, out of a desperation to see God do something real and authentic in our lives and church, we drove a spiritual stake into the spiritual ground as we made this declaration: *"This Day we Fight for what we're Mantled to be!"* This phrase was linked to all those years of warfare that had tried to keep us from our mantle, yet it was this declaration that set the revival *mantle in motion.* We didn't plan to say it, it was a prophetic declaration brought forth by the Spirit with a group of about 75 of our core leaders. The Spirit breathed on it and we acted on it and have been acting on that declaration to this very day.

A declaration is a powerful weapon because life and death are in the power of your tongue. Our declaration came into agreement with the mantle and assignment of sustained revival. And with that we began to fight. Why use the word "fight"? Because there will always be resistance from the enemy in pursuit of revival. The fight will never cease, and neither will we! We won't settle.

We were mantled to be an entry point for revival. A place that hosts a sustained move of the Holy Spirit until Jesus comes back. We were mantled to host Him, not parties that pacify. We were mantled to entertain the Spirit, not people. We were mantled to wait on Him not rush Him. We were mantled to lead people back to the fire of God, at the altar of God, worshipping the One True God. At our moment of declaration, we were finished with status quo, nominal, modern church mentality of *superficial success* and we engaged in a resolve to do whatever it takes for as long as it takes to keep the fire burning on the altar and the door open to revival. With this we began our pursuit of *HIM.*

Chapter Four
The Proof is in the Pursuit

2013 became our year of the pursuit of God. That seems like a no-brainer, but I hope that with the history given in the previous chapter you'll understand why we had to be *intentional* about pursuit. Pursuit is a powerful element in our lives that requires discipline, deliberate focus and effort. We're all pursuing something in life be it leisure, pleasure, education, career-building, a business or raising a family. It's how we're wired and it's not necessarily a bad thing unless we put all other pursuits above our pursuit of Him.

The same is true in building the culture of our churches. We found ourselves placing more hope in building a church by pursuing natural or man-inspired ideas and as a result, they became a substitute for the pure pursuit of His presence. So we began to intentionally emphasize a tenacious, focused pursuit of God and His manifested presence. We took the Psalm of David to heart that says, "My whole being follows hard after You."

I need to emphasize an especially important point here: Do not try to "have revival" without the element of pursuit. A series of services, a guest speaker every now and then, or even more energized services and the like is not revival.

> If the pursuit of Him and Him alone is not the core motivation, it is not revival and it will not last.

These things are not bad or negative in and of themselves, but they are not revival. *If the pursuit of Him and Him alone is not the core motivation, it is not revival and it will not last.*

Two Non-Negotiable Elements of Revival

Although we had preached many sermons on the presence of God, this was our *intentional* turn to go after Him. It was a turn into the "more of God." Little did we know at the time that this year of pursuit would become a primary catalyst and conduit into sustained revival. There is only one entry point for revival and that is when we make the decision to gain more of Him which requires less of me. *The proof of your revival resolve is in your pursuit. The fruit and atmosphere of your life, home, church or church services and structure will show the focus of your pursuit.* This spiritual pursuit paves the way for greater hunger and a spirit of prayer. Prayer and hunger are the very foundation of sustained revival. Absolutely everything related to revival begins and continues with these two non-negotiable elements.

> Prayer and hunger are the very foundation of sustained revival. Absolutely everything related to revival begins and continues with these two non-negotiable elements.

As we saw the atmosphere of the Body of Christ at large get emptier and shallower, we became more disillusioned and disheartened. This led to desperation to see the Lord expose the root of our discouragement with what church had become so He could truly come close, bring His glory and get all the glory. It was really quite simple now that we look back; the root of the digression was embedded in a wrong mentality, misguided ambition and a lack of personal sacrifice. While the *external remedies of growth* were there which satisfied our ambitions, the *inward ache for Him* went into starvation. This is and always will be the root of spiritual barrenness and drought. At some point you must get desperate for more than nominal and press into his supernatural. You are then very close to becoming an entry point for revival.

What I referred to earlier as the "atmosphere shifting over our city" was, I believe, the demonic strongholds tightening the lid on the Holy Spirit in the heavenlies. The *seeker model* of church began to take off in this time period. While we respect the leaders who birthed that concept and the biblical truths that were released, we began to see *Pentecostal* churches, who were birthed in the fire of the Spirit, whose distinctive doctrine is the baptism in the Holy Ghost, who needed to be more aggressive and vocal in the things of the Spirit, *dialing things back* to come into alignment with that model and concept.

Methods and movements came on the scene seemingly one after another with paradigms causing Pentecostal churches to water down messages, take repentance and holiness out of their verbiage, and compromise the altar experience with the moving of the Holy Spirit and His gifts all for the sake of convenience, not offending people, and the gaining of numbers and dollars. Part of the mandate of building a revival culture is to *say no* to anything that competes for the Holy Spirit's time. We don't want *punycost*, we want *Pentecost*, as Lou Engle has said. We want the fullness of the Spirit and whatever he chooses to bring.

My good friend and amazing pastor, Rick Shelton said, the Lord spoke to him in a season of spiritual decline in his church in St. Louis and told him, *"You cannot want Me and not want what I do."* While I do not support out of control weirdness in a church service, I also do not support a man-made schedule and structure that leaves no room for Holy Spirit. To build and sustain a revival culture we must rid ourselves of the lie that modern culture doesn't want the Holy Spirit and what He brings to our lives and corporate gatherings

We must be careful not to redefine what began in the Spirit in an Upper Room on the day of Pentecost and try to finish it in the flesh in boardrooms and planning rooms. It will never work. God will see to it. The only thing that makes the Church relevant to this world is the presence of God. To really let God be God and let Him touch people, our services must become less mechanical and predictable and more focused on creating an atmosphere for God to move. This starts with a hunger for God alone. This hunger will lead you to your knees because prayer is the only posture that can open the entry point for revival.

We Won't Settle

There was a serious shift in our church atmosphere with our 2013 spiritual pursuit which cultivated a hunger in the hearts of the people that said, "God, at all costs we want more of You." Hunger grows and is contagious. However, it is also offensive to the status quo which is why you must have a revival resolve. Hunger is the sustaining element of revival.

Early in the revival there was a prophetic phrase released in one of our services by our praise and worship team. They eventually wrote an entire song based on that phrase birthed in that moment, "We Won't Settle!" This has become our war cry, our heart's cry and declaration of faith. When you settle for something you lose your resolve to stand for something. The moment we back off in our pursuit of more of God is the moment we settle for where we are, what we have and less than what He has to give us. While the work of the Cross and the power of the Blood is enough to save our sin-sick souls, the levels of glory that can come to us as a result of that same sacrificial Cross require a tenacious pursuit for more. This is where a revival cry differs from a random cry. A revival cry is focused, fervent and has a fight. It is aggressive but at the same time reverent. One thing that it is not is neutral. It will not settle for where it is now because the revival

> A revival cry is focused, fervent and has a fight. It is aggressive but at the same time reverent. One thing that it is not is neutral.

cry understands that just one more raw cry for "more" can release an outpouring that shifts entire regions to fall under the weight of the gospel of the Kingdom of God.

This resolve will carry you; it will sustain revival. Hunger is a non-negotiable element of pure revival. You can have all of the outward "signs" of revival, yet not have an inward, driving hunger for Him. The primary way to keep this from happening is to not settle for what you have, but press into Him to overwhelm you. This is the revival song that was birthed out of our desire for more:

We feel You drawing near so we bow before Your Throne
Increase Your Glory here 'cause You're all we're longing for

What we have is not enough, so won't You come and overwhelm us?
We won't settle!
We won't settle!
For anything less than Your glory
For anything less than Your fullness
For anything less than Your fire!

We Won't Settle
Fresh Start Church Worship

You will NOT have revival without hunger, and you will NOT have hunger without placing the highest priority and value on prayer.

Chapter Five
Year of Prayer

*T*he place of pursuit takes you to the place of prayer.
While warfare will bring you to a place of desperation, it is
the turning to prayer where you'll posture yourself to
become an entry point for revival. At the place of prayer,
revival can be birthed, built and sustained. Sustained revival
takes sustained prayer.

> Sustained revival takes sustained prayer!

Testimonial to the Power of Prayer

A testimony that has touched my life over the years is
that of Jackson Senyonga from Uganda. His explanation and
impartation on the power of prayer have radically altered my
approach and priority to it. Following is a quote from his

testimony of how prayer turned *devastation into revival* in Uganda:

> "Uganda used to be the flower or pearl of Africa. When Ediamen took over everything changed. We were dying. Neighbors killed during the night. You couldn't run away from the city because of road blocks and they would kill you. The airports were restricted, it was impossible to escape. We lived not knowing what to do. In our desperation the devil made us pray. See, revival comes to us either from desperation or devastation. We choose the way we want our revival. People in Uganda began to pray like dying people. These are the kinds of prayers that bring revival, not casual prayers. Prayer was not an event for us, it was a lifestyle. We put demands on heaven to open and on the heart of God to respond. Prayer must be taken to that melting point. This wasn't an organized prayer…it was jungle praying (out in the jungle) in the middle of the night and crying out all night long only to return in the morning with insect bites all over them…but they didn't care. Their hunger for God transcended their natural comfort. It was either God came…or they were dead! Transformation came to Uganda because of the fervent praying. Prayer must be able to outcry the sin of the land before revival comes! When the sin of the

city is crying louder than the voice of intercession, we will never see a new day of transformation. In America, you are accustomed to events; therefore, you do not know how fervent prayer can be sustained. Event praying is hit and run praying and when we run the enemy is occupying. Those prayers do not bring revival. But in Uganda we prayed everyday for over 15 years and would not take no for an answer. We reached the melting point of prayer and God answered and it affected the political system, the market place and the church of Uganda. Today there is a new atmosphere in Uganda. Prayer is everywhere…in the State House; the parliament; the judicial system; the market place; on all levels of society – prayer has covered our nation. 15-20 Muslims gave their life to Jesus every week. AIDS has gone from 24% to 8%. Our church went from a few people to thousands in two weeks. We kept extending and extending our building because revival never gave us the opportunity to have a building committee."

There are many choices on how to build your church. While many may lead to the quickest path to growth, revival requires that we consistently and aggressively do the hard work of prayer. Prayer not only rivals but supersedes the results of human ingenuity that appeals to fleshly appetites. While there are methods and approaches that may bring quick growth to your church, prayer is eternal and produces the supernatural weight and substance.

Prayer – Fulcrum of the Church

My quest is the weight of His glory. When people are drawn to the Church may they be drawn by the weight of His glory and not merely a temporal attraction to keep their attention. *If the weight of His glory is your quest, then prayer will be your priority.* The Lord spoke the word "fulcrum" to me one morning upon waking up. I opened my eyes and this word popped into my mind. Unaware of the exact meaning I began to research it.

> If the weight of His glory is your quest, then prayer will be your priority.

Here is the definition: *Fulcrum is the supporting point of a lever, the point on which it pivots. It is something that plays an essential role or serves as the center of an activity or situation. Fulcrum is the person or thing that everything else depends on, the one who can make it work or happen, the one with the answer and solution. Some* synonyms for fulcrum are: guide, core, nucleus, hub, and heart. A fulcrum helps to bear the load, balance the load and distribute the load of a thing.

I felt the Holy Spirit say, "Prayer *is the FULCRUM for the Church!*" Prayer serves as the center of spiritual activity upon which everything else depends. Prayer is what makes things happen and work. Prayer has the answer and solution because it is a direct path to God. Because prayer is the fulcrum for the Church, private and corporate prayer should be the core and nucleus in our personal lives and our corporate gatherings and it should be the hub and heart of the vision of our churches. *FULCRUM! There are no shortcuts. Prayer cannot be an option, it must be the optimal choice.*

Two scriptures, of many, show us the power of prayer that lie within our grasp as a blood-bought believer: Matthew 16:19 in the Amplified Bible says, "I will give you the keys (authority) of the kingdom of heaven; and whatever you bind [forbid, declare to be improper and unlawful] on earth will have [already] been bound in heaven, and whatever you loose [permit, declare lawful] on earth will have [already] been loosed in heaven."

Ephesians 3:20 in the Amplified Bible says, "Now to Him who is able to [carry out His purpose and] do superabundantly more than all that we dare ask or think [infinitely beyond our greatest prayers, hopes, or dreams], according to His power that is at work *within* us..."

Both of these scriptures show us that God partners with our prayers to bring about His purposes. *Prayer is the element that unlocks dimensions of revival and sustains the revival culture.* Prayer raises the spiritual standard corporately, sets the atmosphere, alters outcomes and moves the hand of God. Prayer must be and remain at the helm.

> Prayer is the element that unlocks dimensions of revival and sustains the revival culture.

Revival is birthed and sustained by a praying church. There are certain key elements that *MUST* be adhered to in order *to* sustain a revival culture, and prayer is at the very top of the list. It must consume us as pastors, church leaders and entire congregations. You must commit to building a culture of prayer which is more than a prayer meeting, prayer team or prayer ministry. It must be the *pervading environment* of your church. *You literally become a House of Prayer!*

Prayer Culture is Foundational to Revival Culture

As we became intentional about building a revival culture, we knew that we had to increase prayer personally and corporately. The Lord showed me that *He could build no higher (spiritually) than the depth and width of our prayer foundation. Revival is a spiritual pursuit, not another man-made model or structure from the "how to do church" manual.* Because of this, prayer must permeate every aspect of your life and church, it must be prioritized. As said by Samuel Chadwick, "The one concern of the devil is to keep the saints from praying. He laughs at our toil, mocks at our wisdom, but trembles when we pray."

The *prayer culture* took off for us in 2014 when we were willing to take a risk and shift our traditional Wednesday night activities and structure to accommodate and prioritize one *large weekly corporate worship and prayer gathering.* These gatherings we call "GAP," God Answers Prayer. We were not aware of the scope of spiritual growth in revival that we were moving into as we made prayer a priority. We began to meet as a staff to fast and pray every Wednesday and Thursday at noon and that commitment continues to this day. We consistently followed the bread crumbs of the Holy Spirit, as I would call it. A crumb here and there would be set before us as we persevered in prayer. These spiritual crumbs were leading us and sustaining us in revival.

We bring all ages together for our GAP prayer service from babies to seniors for worship and intercession. As we made this shift, we began to see a greater interest and response in prayer, people grow in prayer and we begin to see prayer grow in the people. Your church schedule and your personal schedule will reflect if prayer is a priority. Jesus prioritized prayer as did the first-century church. Why shouldn't we? Why don't we? I'm concerned that we've moved the boundary lines by our distraction with non-essentials and compromised the revival culture by placing less emphasis on corporate prayer.

People will come to corporate prayer when taught that it is a *core value and a non-negotiable element of their personal lives and their revival church culture.* Jesus said, "My Father's house shall be called a house of prayer for all nations…" Yet we've managed to make it a house of everything but prayer. When people see that we value and esteem corporate prayer they will gain a different perspective of the prayer services. We tell our people that our Wednesday night GAP is the most important meeting of the week and we mean it. When they hear us say this, it transmits to them the value of corporate prayer. On our journey we have found that *revival will come and revival will stay…IF we pray!*

Building Spiritual People sustains Revival

One of the key decisions in building a culture of revival is that you have to be committed to building *a spiritual house.* The Word of God says; "But I say, walk by the Spirit, and you will not carry out the desire of the flesh. For the flesh sets its desire against the Spirit, and the Spirit against the flesh; for these are in opposition to one another, so that you may not do the things that you please. (Galatians 5:16-17 NASB) *The people of a revival church must be spiritual and prayer is where it begins.* To carry a culture of revival, the carnality of flesh must be challenged. If we speak truth concerning the hindrances of flesh, and we point people toward personal prayer, the spiritual bar will rise in their lives.

We must love to pray, and many will not learn to love to pray until they have a revelation of the power of prayer. When our churches can see transformation in the lives of people and transformation of the atmospheres of our services and their homes, they will be encouraged in their praying knowing that it is shifting things in the spirit realm and in earthly atmospheres, including their homes and cities.

Praying people build a spiritual atmosphere that challenges the status-quo and low-level spiritual pursuit. We have labored diligently to teach our people to recognize when religious devils want to steal our corporate revival atmosphere. Praying people discern the enemies of revival and take authority over them in the spirit to release the atmosphere of the Holy Ghost – this is a vital part of the revival culture. Our goal isn't just more people rather, we want to build SPIRITUAL people who build a SPIRITUAL house. If we will throw our efforts into the essential revival *element of prayer*, the Holy Spirit will begin to expand and shift the hearts of people which expands and shifts the spiritual atmosphere which begins to build and sustain a culture of revival.

It is my concern that some of the systems and strategies we use to build our churches limit the spiritual capacity in people and produce a carnal church with only spiritual talking points. We have arrived in a church culture where the most that is being built is a convenient and comfortable environment for people to have the choice of things like; multiple services, shorter services, sermons that are palatable and primarily earthly, and membership assimilation that seems to be more about information rather than spiritual impartation. Within these strategies there is little to no transfer of the reality of the sacrificial spiritual price required for an authentic move of God. *Revival will never be convenient or comfortable. Revival cannot fit into one box or even our mindsets. Revival requires placing a priority on what Holy Spirit wants and needs to do.*

> Revival will never be convenient or comfortable. Revival cannot fit into one box or even our mindsets.

Revival always has the price tag of sacrifice attached to it. Therefore, building a people of prayer is essential to them grasping these spiritual principles of revival. If we fail to do so, they will wear out and eventually leave because flesh never likes sacrifice. However, when you are saturated with prayer, it changes how you see everything.

Revival Is Always Preceded by Prayer

Our year of pursuit was the beginning of a spirit of revival, our year of prayer resulted in the outbreak of revival which has led to a sustained culture of revival. The birthing of the revival spirit through prayer sustains a perpetual hunger for revival. This is priceless. *There is no other thing that can bring spiritual hunger, only spending time with the Lord.* When hunger is the pervasive sound of an atmosphere, it becomes contagious to the believer and curious to the unbelievers. When the world walks into our churches they should sense and feel an atmosphere of spiritual hunger for God. We don't need to downplay His presence, push pause on the moving of His Holy Spirit to reach the unreached. The Word of God says that His presence brings *fullness* and fullness is revival. It is also what the unbeliever is searching for. Their empty hearts can become *full of His Spirit* as they encounter Him in a culture of revival.

Because revival is much more than just an outward excitement or energy, building people through prayer and spiritual encounter is essential. Failing to do so will bring a lack of spiritual substance and spiritual authority. Any amount of the manifestation of the Spirit that you have will be short-lived. Shouts will ring shallow and crescendo music will fall short of the manifested glory. Revival is cultivated in a heart and then emanates through every aspect of that life. Our failure to cultivate deep, passionate, aggressive spiritual hunger for God results in shallow Christianity that settles for shallow churches. When human carnality goes unchallenged it will go unchanged. We mustn't accept carnal Christianity and believe that God winks and overlooks. He does not!

One of the greatest travesties is an unchallenged and unchanged heart.

Carnality is a Barrier to Revival

So, unfortunately, carnality is a great hindrance to corporate revival and is rampant today among believers. Anyone of us at any moment can succumb to carnality. However, in a revival culture it is something that cannot be allowed to overthrow the pervasive atmosphere of spiritual pursuit. Carnality greatly affects our corporate atmospheres because it means you live in the *natural more than the spiritual.* Consequently, it dictates how you view everything. The only way to get carnality out is to grow spiritually and this is where intentional prayer and *revival discipleship* comes in: *Everyone must give themselves to spiritual pursuit, to knowledge, wisdom, revelation and the spiritual experiences that revival brings.*

Everyone must give themselves to spiritual pursuit, to knowledge, wisdom, revelation and the spiritual experiences that revival brings.

People should be taught that a personal daily sacrifice is required to maintain their spiritual fire. As people sell out to spiritual pursuit, their perspective, priorities and values change. The result is they will cease making carnal choices and begin to clearly see *the spiritual realm and its impact on their lives and families.*

The primary way we saw this shift happen was through our continual challenge of saturating people in personal and corporate prayer. We were intentional to teach that the move of God and spiritual pursuit is a priority. Desperation to see God's glory will cause you to do things that go against the popular *crowd and culture* and to *break the mold...*this is where revivalists and revival churches must live.

Children in Revival

A significant thing for our church during this season was watching prayer not only grow in the adults but also in the *children and youth.* Our children's pastor became intentional about praying with and allowing the children to pray during kid's church. She challenged the children's leaders and parents of the children to be intentional about prayer before service, which they called "Pre-heat Prayer". She began to gather the kids, parents and leadership early before start time to pray with them. This was the beginning of what is now a thriving pre-service prayer meeting that has built an army of children who are Holy Ghost baptized intercessors.

At this same time, the youth leadership began to change what prayer looked like in the youth ministry. They also began pre-service prayer to place more responsibility on the youth for setting the atmosphere for their own service. They wanted to increase their hunger for spiritual things so that every time they met together, they would encounter the presence of God.

It started with our youth leaders leading the prayer while recorded music played in the background. They began to teach the youth how to pray at greater levels. Little did we know that the Holy Spirit was orchestrating and aligning us for *a revival that would break out* using these teenage and young adult prayer warriors just one year later.

The youth ministry pre-service prayer grew to such a point that a live band began to play in the background to assist the prophetic flow. The youth would pray leading by microphone until the atmosphere became electric and conducive for the glory of the Lord. This model is now used to open all of our services. When people walk into our church they walk into a prayer meeting. After all, isn't His house supposed to be a house of prayer?

It is a fact that most people rise only to the level to which they are challenged. In our season of pursuit, the people had to be *challenged* to be and stay hungry. In our season of establishing a house of prayer, the same was true, the people had to be challenged to pray and continue to pray. Because the prevailing mentality of most church-goers is to just come and do church for a few minutes during the week, a great spiritual challenge is needed that says; "Do you want more of God?" Believers with any level of desire for the Lord would answer, yes! However, many times our lifestyle choices, priorities, our actions, thought processes and church structures prove otherwise.

When we began to intentionally challenge the spiritual level of our people it brought a shift in our corporate gatherings and a lift in our prayer culture. When we began to push them to greater *spiritual intensity, we began to see growth in the spirit of prayer* that wasn't out of duty but a desperation and desire to have more and experience more of God.

The prevailing atmosphere at our corporate prayer service is charged with a strong presence and an aggressive, passionate spiritual pursuit. Our prayer mantle has extended to governmental intercession for nations. This has evolved as God has strengthened our spirits to continue to expand in spiritual authority. The pervasive atmosphere of our gatherings is spiritual aggression or intensity. Some people are turned off by this and to them I ask why? Prayer brings us into an attitude of non-negotiable passion for Jesus and His Kingdom purpose. You can't tame that…I don't want tame prayer.

> Prayer brings us into an attitude of non-negotiable passion for Jesus and His Kingdom purpose. You can't tame that…I don't want tame prayer.

If I Can Teach You to Love to Pray

We are committed to teaching our people to *love to pray* because if I can teach you to love to pray, revival is inevitable and the outcome is limitless. When we love to pray, the corporate and personal spiritual growth never stops. Our prayers are supernatural seeds that never die, are never forgotten and they never go unanswered. They are incense before the Throne of God that activates Throne room activity into this earthly realm.

May our heart cry be, *Lord, help us love to pray,* because if you to love to pray, you can release destinies 30-50 years from now, open *unending heavenly realms,* call for healing, deliverance, salvation, provision, protection, prosperity, providence, power, and angels armies of heavenly ranks!

If I can teach you to love to pray, you can learn to stand on your own, lay hands on yourself and be set free, learn to persevere and withstand the schemes of the devil! Strongholds will shatter, depression can't imprison you, and rejection can't hold you and sickness must flee from you. If I can teach you to love to pray, I will have taught you to connect and commune with the Lover of your soul, as you will have opened the door of your heart to the Creator of your heart and the One who knows you like no other. If I can teach you to love to pray, you will fall in love with Him and realize that any alternative falls short of your companionship with Him.

If I can teach you to love to pray, you will gain the attention of heaven and you will command the attention of hell! God will use you to birth, shift and establish things in the spirit. He will use you to defeat and displace the works of the enemy in your territory, keeping the ranks of darkness at bay in your region and the lives of the people in that territory will be forever changed because you love to pray. God will use you as an instrument to open the heavens over your family, church, city, region and nation.

As you respond to be gripped by the greater of God in prayer, God will unfold to you what eye has not seen, ear heard nor heart comprehended. He will reveal His secrets to you as your prayers break up the foundations of the fallow ground to unleash the mysteries of God. He will use us to do greater works and exploits for His Kingdom purpose, when you love to pray. You *will* see the miraculous and entire territories bow under the weight of the gospel of Jesus Christ and the power of the Holy Spirit. You *will* see countless lives, pastors, and entire congregations touched by the fire of God and the spirit of revival. *WHEN YOU LOVE TO PRAY!*

The Prayer Foundation Must Go Deep

I mentioned earlier that around 2007 the Holy Spirit spoke something to me along these lines: *"The size of the impact and influence of your church will be determined by the size of your personal and corporate prayer. How much impact do you want to make in this ministry, the Holy Spirit asked? Then your prayer foundation must be bigger, stronger, deeper and wider than that to sustain it, He said."* With that understanding, we should recognize that we will go no higher (in spiritual impact) than the depth of our prayer foundation.

Our weekly GAP prayer service is the fuel to the revival, without it we would be substance-*less and weak,* but with it we continually have the reality of His tangible presence and all of heaven's army behind us as we continue forward in sustained revival. What I knew in part in 2007 has become a *greater revelation* in my life and our ministry. As I look around at the growth, the expansion and most of all the spirit of revival that has transpired over these years, I literally weep and stand in awe at what God has, is and will do as we stay on our knees building that foundation of prayer.

Do not be sidetracked by man-made church growth concepts, their at best a foundation of *sand.* There is only one way to lay a strong spiritual foundation and that is in the place of prayer. This posture of prayer isn't popular because it's found *on your knees; on the floor; face down; no crowds, no pomp and parade.* It's just you, Jesus and the powerful instrument called...PRAYER. Prayer builds an eternal foundation in our lives and our churches. It can never stop being poured out until Jesus comes. It is a perpetual pouring out to maintain an earthly foundation that will transition into an eternal one. And as we do so, we're sustaining revival until Jesus' return.

Hell isn't nervous at our knowledge, our title or our talent, *but* it trembles, it moves out of the way and it must obey blood-bought believers on their knees in prayer! If I teach you a program, system or ideal, at best, I *equip you* with the knowledge of that program, system or ideal and *at the least,* I entertain you with it. But if I can teach you to love to pray you'll then have an entry point for revival. You will have found your Bethel and Peniel and your revival journey has begun, when you love to pray.

> But if I can teach you to love to pray you'll then have an entry point for revival. You will have found your Bethel and Peniel and your revival journey has begun, when you love to pray.

So, if I were the devil, I would make believers lazy in prayer, make them too busy to pray, make them believe that the prayer meeting is the boring meeting, that God doesn't hear nor answer my prayer. If I were the devil, I would cause pastors to run to everything else except the prayer closet and prioritize everything else except the prayer meeting.

It's amazing to think that the twelve disciples had Jesus as a captive life coach for three years. They could have asked Him to teach them absolutely anything but the one lesson that they asked for was: TEACH US TO PRAY! This should show us something about the priority of prayer. As Jesus launched the Church in the book of Acts He sent them UP before He sent them OUT!   Up to a prayer meeting then out to release what they had received.

To summarize: sustainable revival doesn't just come; it's birthed, built and sustained through prayer and spiritual pursuit. As you keep those things alive, the spiritual atmosphere in your life and corporate gatherings will intensify so much that revival will become your culture. There have been mighty outpourings of God in history that have come and gone because there were no doorkeepers. No firekeepers. No one who made sure the move of God was top on the priority list. When you become a doorkeeper of revival you stand in your place of authority to protect and feed the move of God. If you do, it will sustain and you'll continue to see revival fruit and harvest. This all begins and ends with prayer. I trust that I've taught you to *love to pray.*

Chapter Six
Year of the Threshold

*T*he year of 2014 was the birthing of a new level of prayer and it was also the year that we began to intentionally preach about revival, dealing with the theme, the history and the part that prayer plays in preparing for revival. We began to have a laser focus on this subject. One of the ways we kept that focus was to begin to revisit revivals of old. The value of this approach *stirs a desire to see more* than your current experience. If God did it then, He will do it now!

I remember attending a meeting several years before our turn into revival where one of the guest speakers was Pastor John Kilpatrick, the General of the Brownsville revival in the mid-1990s. As he began to tell the stories of revival the hunger began to grow and the tears began to flow. This is what revival will do; it will continually propel you to set the spiritual bar higher. To some, this will be intimidating and for others even seem daunting, but if your hunger remains, you will not settle for anything less.

> This is what revival will do; it will continually propel you to set the spiritual bar higher. To some, this will be intimidating and for others even seem daunting, but if your hunger remains, you will not settle for anything less.

What we didn't understand in that season was that we were *aligning with our assignment* to be a revival center (a strategic place of continual outpouring). We were following our heart and passion but of utmost importance, His heart and His passion. And as we were seeking Him, He was blessing us and gracing us as we took steps of faith into revival destiny. We can look back and see how the "1-2-3's" were being put together by the Lord. All of these significant changes took place little by little as we pursued Him, pressing into revival and trying to follow His voice and direction with every decision. Each change we made was intimidating in the natural because it drifted farther away from our comfort zones, but each change brought us closer to destiny and to *revival.*

Non-negotiable elements

In the early part of 2015 we hired a church consultant because we still desired to learn to make the church healthy. There were a number of valuable things that we learned from him that helped us be better leaders and build a stronger infrastructure in our church. However, we quickly realized was that even though this consulting ministry professed to embrace the moving of the Spirit, their foundational methods still followed modern church growth techniques. Methods that leave little to no room for the placing of priority on the moving of the Holy Spirit or the tangible manifestation of the presence of God *in* your services.

These methods included: shorter services, multiple services, multi-sites, shorter sermons, no altars and only allow Holy Spirit baptism in a private or semi-private setting. For a revival culture, *ALL* of these are non-negotiable! *Most church growth methods meant to lead you to bigger numbers lead to a smaller Holy Spirit.* We had to come to the resolve that whatever we did we would not compromise giving Holy Spirit time to move in the way He wanted to move. We would not compromise preaching truth and we definitely would not *remove the altar* from the House of God. I would like to be very clear that I do not feel that all of these methods he taught are necessarily wrong, but if they lead you to a limitation in the place of encounter in your life or the life of your church services then I do believe that our motivation is wrong.

I must say in the defense of this church consultant, after revival broke out at our church, he gave us a very key and strategic statement that we have clung to in building a strong, sustained revival culture and it is this: *We build the structure of our church around the move of God.* Revival can't be built around other things. Other things must be built around revival.

> We build the structure of our church around the move of God. Revival can't be built around other things. Other things must be built around revival.

If there is a key component to what we have to say based on our experience it would be: *Revival must be your main focus. There can be no plan B!*

In Revival's Threshold

In 2015 we held a special Pentecost Sunday service with Pastor John Kilpatrick. This was his first visit to our church. He released a personal word to my husband and me that our church was *in the threshold of revival.* This was hugely impactful to us as a General of revival recognized the spirit of revival stirring in our church. His statement carried great weight as we moved forward the next few months.

We began to pray and preach into crossing that threshold. If we were in it then we needed to cross over! Within just a few months, in August of 2015, *revival broke out!* The catalyst was our youth and young adult conference. Isaiah Saldivar, our guest speaker that weekend, declared on the last night of the conference (not knowing what Pastor John Kilpatrick had said to us personally); *"this church has just gone through the threshold!"*

At the end of the final service, during the altar time, I said to my husband that I felt we were to call the people back for the next Sunday night to continue this meeting. We asked Isaiah if he could return to be our guest and he not only returned for just one Sunday night but for many more after that. In fact, *for 52 Sunday nights we continued revival* and *the spirit of revival kept growing and growing.*

We had now reached a point where the consecration, prayer and sacrifice were building more and more spiritual momentum. God was drastically changing lives, souls were being saved, countless people baptized in the Holy Ghost in the altars, new people were coming to the church but the most powerful element at that point was the work that God was doing in the lives *of those already in the church.*

With the assignment of a revival center that He was giving us, and the revival mantle He had placed on us, He knew we would need *an army* that would be forerunners to forge forward into the unchartered waters of sustained revival. In the seasons ahead it would require many Aarons' and Hurs' who would hold up our arms as the battle for perpetual fire raged. Each of these people are precious and valuable and they are those who are charged with a *warrior spirit* and *a Holy Ghost revival fire.* They are firebrands who came alongside us to be doorkeepers of revival!

Crossing the Red Sea of Revival

As you desire revival there is one thing that should be learned; how to cross thresholds. Throughout our revival, our intercessory cry has brought us to many strategic, spiritual thresholds. Intercession will *propel* you forward in revival and with that will come continual spiritual thresholds that must be faced and crossed. If not, you will stifle. At these thresholds there can be no negotiation about continuing in revival. Trust me, you will be challenged, greatly.

You must have built an impenetrable revival resolve to continue crossing over. I feel the reason many churches, pastors and believers cannot sustain revival is because they don't understand the importance of having an unshakable revival resolve. At every spiritual threshold we were met with significant demonic resistance that we were not always ready for or expecting. However, this journey of revival resolve has taught us how to press in and breakthrough critical resistance until the glory is released and you cross over.

Thresholds are places we come to where we either go forward or backward. They are places where decisions must be made, battles must be fought and transition must happen in order to cross over into greater capacity. They are places where pain tolerance is built and spiritual authority is identified. Thresholds are places of graduating to the *next* and if you don't learn how to cross, you'll be stalled.

This, I believe, is what happens much of the time to leaders as they try to lead congregations across the *Red Sea of revival* and the thresholds become more challenging. This challenge can be daunting if you're not spiritually ready for it. But we need to understand that when we cross one threshold of revival, no matter the sacrifice or warfare, we're stronger, more discerning and more graced to cross the next one. This is the journey of sustained revival – learn to cross thresholds. Don't stand in them, back away from them or try to negotiate a way around them…in faith, cross over!

> This is the journey of sustained revival - learn to cross thresholds. Don't stand in them, back away from them or try to negotiate a way around them...in faith, cross over!

2015 was the year revival broke out. I remind you of our declaration just two short years before: *"This day we fight for what we're mantled to be!"* In August of that year we put on the mantle. The fight hasn't stopped but the mantle grows ever stronger and beautiful. God has a revival mantle for you and it's worth the fight, sacrifice and process to be a doorkeeper of revival.

Chapter Seven
Year of Identity

*A*fter revival hit in 2015, we quickly realized that our church structure had to change again. Remember, we're building the structure around the move of God. I want to pause for a moment in the flow of our story and emphasize the importance of this chapter in our journey. If you do not make room for revival in your personal life and your church structure, revival will just become another option. Keeping in mind the definition we began with for revival: the sustained presence and power of God that results in transformation. To sustain the presence and power of God, there must be a wineskin that supports that goal.

Revival cannot be an add-on to other good ideals, it must be all-consuming. For this to happen in a sustained manner, especially within a local church body, it must become your identity and structure must be built around that. Revival demands sacrifice and one of the first things we noticed in our turn into revival was the limitations of our traditional or popular structures. The Lord began to lead us, even before we knew what we were doing, about shifting the structure of our church to accommodate the move of God, this included service schedule, small groups and much more. *Don't be afraid to build your structure around the move of God instead of building a structure and hoping God moves within what you've built. Shift the structure to build a spiritual house. This brings the reward of His presence, His sustained presence and sustained revival.*

> Don't be afraid to build your structure around the move of God instead of building a structure and hoping God moves within what you've built. Shift the structure to build a spiritual house. This brings the reward of His presence, His sustained presence and sustained revival.

As I share some of the changes that supported the revival identity, apply this to your personal life as well as a corporate church setting.

Will You Break the Mold for Revival?

Significant changes began in 2016. The decision was made to continue our revival every Sunday night. This meant we had to do something with the youth, children and small groups that we had previously moved from Wednesday night.

I feel *very strongly* that structures and systems *can* become a great hindrance to sustained revival culture in the local church. I am not saying that we should not have them, but I am saying that they should not have us at their mercy and compromise revival. In this season, we felt it was a test to see if we were going to be *okay* with *not looking like the trendy or the traditional church.* The Holy Spirit spoke to us in one of our staff prayer meetings and gave us permission to *"break the mold."* Because most every church looked the same, our *assignment* was quickly forcing us to *choose the mantle over methods.* That said, no matter what the change, *you can't be afraid to look different to sustain revival.* This goes for anything that does not fit the assignment of revival. Multiple church campuses, even multiple services may not fit what you're supposed to do. You can't be afraid to look different. You've got to be willing to sacrifice a program or ministry to *sustain revival. "I give you permission to break the mold!"* That statement given by the Holy Spirit equipped and propelled us into a stronger resolve to sustain revival.

For our youth ministry the first two things they sacrificed for revival were a weekly youth service and small groups for *four* months! The Lord honored that sacrifice, especially through those initial stages. But the most rewarding aspect of this element was that the youth didn't seem to mind! They were, and still are, major catalysts of this revival. Because of their passion, they grew to accept and prioritize the moving of the Holy Spirit *and* the assignment of revival for our church. This is an indescribable blessing to a senior pastor. So many are trying to figure out how to reach youth and young adults these days, we have found that they are looking for the real, authentic presence and power of God. They are looking for revival.

As the months pressed on, we're only one year into this move of God, we came together as a staff and decided that we would pursue a revival culture that would run through *every ministry* of the church. Revival would be the thread that runs through every aspect of who we are. *Remember, the Holy Spirit gave us permission to "break the mold". This is who we are and this is what we do - Revival.*

What Are We Going To Go Back To?

We had many discussions where we would consider; *"Where are we going with this?" "What is this going to look like in the future?"* The inference was, *"Are we ever going back to the way it used to be?" "Are we going back to the old structure?"* The old flow? The old way we operated? In one of those critical discussions, our worship pastor, Jessica Schlueter, said, *"What are we going to go back to?"*

This is a valuable question to ask as you consider birthing, building and sustaining a revival culture. *The reality is that once you've tasted more you have no desire to go back to normal or nominal.*

We were *searching for definition and identity* of what the future of *sustained revival* would look like in our church. It's easy to see now because hindsight is 20/20. However, when you're pioneering you only see what's in front of you, and that's a blank slate. We knew of no church that pursued continual revival and held the paradigm of a sustained move of God.

As revival was increasing in momentum, we had to make a decision if and how we were going to keep it moving forward in its current state. Our *revival resolve was being shaped and molded in our hearts.* We held a conviction that the Spirit led us to where we were and we could not be *afraid* of never going back. *This is a key if you're going to sustain a revival culture.*

> When you automatically assume that revival is only for a season, you will not go all in nor will you change structure to accommodate it.

When you automatically assume that revival is only for a season, you will not go all in nor will you change structure to accommodate it.

Revival has to be *the* plan and not *one* of the plans. Revival isn't another model or ideal and it's definitely not a fad. Revival is relationship and spiritual pursuit. Revival is a spiritual move of the Holy Spirit that arrests all else and forces your focus on Him and His agenda alone. Revival will change the entire landscape of your life and church. So, if you go into it with the paradigm that this is temporary, or that you just want to have a few good services to build spiritual momentum, then there is a good chance you will go back to normal and nominal; the place of no revival fire and average spiritual pursuit.

Here is a very important point: Revival comes first into hearts of people then people will support revival services. While a single service or meeting can help as a catalyst, the hearts of people must be prepared to support the increased spiritual capacity that revival structure brings. Meetings and services are powerful and much needed; however, the fuel behind them will always be the spiritual hunger in the hearts of the people. Continual cultivation of this is crucial to sustained revival. So, you must ask yourself the difficult questions: What am I building around? What do I really want to produce in my life and in my church?

Revival culture is built around the presence of God. King David put the presence of God where the people were. Davidic worship requires that the presence be put in the forefront not behind a curtain or outside the camp or in a back room on an "off night". People are important, very important, but they must experience the presence of God to experience true change. A revival culture must *sustain* a high level of Holy Spirit presence that leads unto transformation. If this is going to happen, His presence must be *given precedence in our structures and revival must be considered our only option.*

Growing from Glory to Glory Is Sustained Revival

When you preach and teach *revival* the people are given seeds of hunger for more than nominal church and nominal

Christian lifestyle and become open to any change that will facilitate it. Through this process, the people have to know that if they are truly chasing God, He's not going to remain in one spot. In revival we *grow* from *glory to glory*. Not only must we continue to grow with revival individually but also corporately. *If you don't grow with revival it will outgrow you.*

> In revival we *grow* from *glory to glory*. Not only must we continue to grow with revival individually but also corporately. *If you don't grow with revival, it will outgrow you.*

So, as an individual, one must stay hungry. As a spiritual leader of a revival church, one must do whatever it takes to sustain the momentum of the Spirit even if that means losing some mindsets and structures that are limiting the move of the Holy Spirit. God looks at us to see how committed we are to the pursuit. Many are afraid if they upset their structure that people will not respond and stop coming.

The reality is that most will embrace something new if they understand that you're not doing it to *make* something happen but *BECAUSE* something is happening. If you're just changing things for the sake of changing things, due to a lack of momentum, people get tired of that. But if the spirit of revival is pushing you to change a structure or system because of time and space needed to accommodate His Presence and the altar, then the risk is well worth it and those with willing hungry hearts will embrace it.

I would add, however, that not all will go with you. Revival confronts carnality and the status-quo. Revival constantly raises the spiritual bar and the press, push and contending that must accompany sustained revival will challenge every spiritual and natural fiber of people's lives. It must be understood that not everyone wants to make the sacrifice and not all are up to the challenge. Not everyone will want to change. However, the risk is worth it. You are building the Church that Jesus wants and preaching the Kingdom like Jesus preached. You are freely allowing spiritual encounters and openly refusing to allow humanistic structure and mentalities to overrun *revival*. To sustain revival, the fear of man must bow to the fear of the Lord. Break the mold for the sake of His presence.

> To sustain revival, the fear of man must bow to the fear of the Lord. Break the mold for the sake of His presence.

When you have the wind of God's Spirit blowing in the atmosphere the people will not resist it! If God's spirit is touching people, God will be moving in their hearts which will make any change not only warranted but also wanted.

The *standard of the Spirit* that was birthed in the early church came out of their Upper Room experience and gave them the blueprint for *The Church*. This blueprint hasn't changed, we have changed it, but Jesus never did. What He began with is what He wants to end with on this earth! The teachings of Jesus, along with their upper room Spirit encounter was a deposit within and as they came out of the Upper Room, they came out with a Spirit-birthed, spirit-filled plan that dictated everything they did from that point on.

Use the Upper Room Strategy for Revival

The Acts blueprint and the upper room standard of the Spirit made them strong in: preaching the Word, giving and generosity, knowing the Word, making disciples, the fellowship of koinonia, and *all* of these were *Spirit-birthed and Spirit-filled*. Everything that you need to be a Spirit-filled believer and church is already laid out in the Word. I'm not sure why feel we need to improve on that. We should ask ourselves, if it's not Spirit-birthed then is it really that important?

This is where you must begin; revival has to be birthed in your own *spirit by finding your own upper room.* I told you that in 2014, we made an upper room at our church on Wednesday nights. This became our conception, birthing, delivery and strategy room and still is today. Every pastor must make an upper room for their congregation and every believer must make an upper room for their life. The last thing we want to do with revival is to make it just another plan or model.

> The last thing we want to do with revival is to make it just another plan or model.

We have lots of plans but all we need *spirit-birthed strategy* in each church that brings God's agenda into that atmosphere. No matter how creative and even successful a human plan is, it will always be mechanical. In other words, it just becomes something that you "work" to get a desired result. On the other hand, an *upper room prayer* will always be *miraculous. Mechanical or miraculous?* I choose miraculous because it will always have the touch of the Spirit. Be aware that you will always fight digressing to the mechanical and to combat this *you must always keep an upper room.*

If you're going to have a revival culture it will take changing structure and paradigms and it will also take *time.* It will not happen instantly in today's microwave mentality. In our personal journey in sustained revival, every change we made to accommodate revival was well thought through, prayed over extensively, and discussed as a staff for quite some time before each decision was made. We made no random decisions that just sounded like a good idea.

I want to make sure that I add, as you read our journey, pray about what God is speaking for your life, for your congregation, for your city. There are many non-negotiable elements, but how and when you implement change is very important to the success of sustained revival.

You must concentrate on consistently building spiritual people and spiritual atmospheres and that takes time, energy, investment and process and much, much prayer. I encourage you to count the cost, and then do whatever it takes, for as long as it takes to keep the door open to revival and the fire burning on the altar!

Don't Try Programming Holy Spirit

For a corporate setting, please understand that the moving of the Spirit isn't going to happen in our well-ordered, controlled services. I fully realize that some will argue this point, and that is fine. But, if we're truly honest, our tight schedules and mini services have produced very little time for people to encounter God. We decided that after revival broke out in August of 2015, and after having several years of two Sunday morning services, we would change our Sunday morning structure in January 2016 to *one Sunday morning service.*

The benefit of one service over multiple services is that you're not restricted. Of all the changes we made to accommodate the move of God, this was the most effective for the purpose of *sustained revival.* By allowing more time in the service, we were able to cultivate a freer atmosphere, allow the Spirit to move as He desired and prioritize altars and spiritual encounters. Not to mention that the delivery of the Word wasn't bound to a countdown clock and worship wasn't restricted to an allotted amount of time.

I'm convinced that our modern methods haven't only *taken out* Holy Spirit but also an element of *reverence for the House of God.* In our effort to become more convenience-driven for people and to accommodate their preferences we have lost the ability to tarry, linger and listen to the Holy Spirit. *It's in and out.* That's what it's all about. Yes, we've developed an in-and-out mentality. (In-N-Out is a *fast-food chain* in the western part of the USA). This mentality says;

"get me in and out as fast as you can, feed me quickly, doesn't matter if it's healthy, just something that tastes good." This mentality doesn't want inconvenience or anything that will complicate schedules. This attitude isn't reverence; this is *spiritual laziness and compromise.*

By way of common sense allow me to say that I certainly understand that some churches cannot accommodate their entire crowd in one service due to a lack of seating or possibly parking issues. However, this isn't the case for most churches. We often use multiple services as an exterior prestige to make us look like we're larger than we really are when most of the services are scarcely full. It is not my intent to say that all cases for multiple services are wrong. However, if you're building a revival culture, even if you must have multiple services, you must arrange the times where Holy Spirit has *His* time, *His* way and *His* agenda. *Spirit sensitive* is the way we should view it.

Other benefits of one service are that you're able to have prophetic flow in praise and worship and more practically, you're not exhausting your staff and volunteers. Trying to do two services in a revival culture is entirely different than when you're doing 55 minutes services with 22 min of worship and 10 min of announcements and 23-

minute sermons. You can do that all day long and not wear out. But when you're pressing into the prophetic, pushing back powers of darkness and displacing principalities, contending for the energy of the Spirit, breakthrough and moving people to a place of supernatural encounter; that takes a spiritual energy for everyone involved. It's important to understand that *in a typical revival*

> *Revival is not planned, prompted, performed, perfected or scripted, it's cultivated and then released.*

culture service, when "it's released…it's released". Revival is not planned, prompted, performed, perfected or scripted, it's cultivated and then released.

The prayer that you've put into that service has *BIRTHED* something for *THAT* service, for that time and those people present. *The point is, that you cannot reproduce revival in multiple services.* Now, you can go into another service and "start all over again", but you cannot duplicate the previous service. Once that anointing is cultivated and released…it's released!

The contrast is with structured, mechanical services that have no Holy Spirit flow, can be easily duplicated and what much of the church has become today. To sustain a revival culture, you cannot lean on your own understanding or someone else's for that matter, nor lean on a talent or program; you *must* rely on the Spirit. *Each service has to be birthed in the upper room.*

The Multiple Service Problem

In multiple services different atmospheres that are generated by the diversity of people present along with other spiritual variables. People who come are at different spiritual levels that affect the atmosphere. This is why it is important to have your key people present in your revival service to push, press and cultivate the spiritual atmosphere. *Atmosphere is everything* and with multiple services there will always be a *constraint on the atmosphere* because of time and the varied spiritual levels of people who attend each service.

This is the reason one service works so well for a revival culture because it builds and then releases according to the Holy Spirit's standard and flow. As stated, it's difficult to replicate this in multiple services.

As a revival church, if you don't have your praisers, intercessors, and mature worshippers present, the atmosphere of freedom is not going to be generated. There is no way you can get around that fact. To keep the atmosphere conducive to revival, you must have the contenders and the intercessors pushing and pressing on behalf of those who don't know or understand how to do so.

Those who are less mature (sinner or immature believer) have to be absorbed into the revival atmosphere because they don't have *the capacity to create it*. This was the roadblock that we ran into with multiple services. We are revivalists who preach revival, have prophetic worship and open altars, who linger and allow His presence to manifest. This is who we are, however, if you have another service with people coming in who are not carrying that spiritual desire or capacity then you're not able to create the revival atmosphere. So, if a revival culture is what you want to build then you have to take all of these elements concerning atmosphere into serious consideration. We believe this is a key principle for sustained revival.

When the congregation is all together in one mind and one accord and in one place it makes that *moment* more impactful. You're never able to get a "moment" back. It cannot be duplicated. Multiple services automatically put God and the things He wants to release into a box. The attitude becomes: "It was awesome, Lord, what You did in the last service, let's see if we can open that back up and let it happen again." *This will not happen & cannot happen, because the people who helped generate that atmosphere just left and a new crop of people are coming in that haven't been in the flow, have different degrees of spirituality & will need a different level of leadership in worship and preaching.*

This became ever so apparent to us when there was a powerful prophetic flow in the first service and people coming into the second service walked in on a *full-blown* move of the Spirit that had been cultivated the last two hours but they were *out of the loop* because they had not been there. It was obvious as a revival church we all needed to be together as one, let a revival atmosphere be released, and let God do whatever He wants to do without any restraints.

A critical point concerning multiple services is that without realizing it, you are actually creating multiple churches, dividing the church on purpose. The Early Church came out of that room as ONE because they were in ONE place TOGETHER! Think about if they had decided to do "two" upper rooms that day? I know that's a far stretch, but I believe worth considering. Yes, the Spirit can be poured out at any moment on any people. But the *KEY point I am pressing on is cultivation of atmosphere.*

The KEY point is cultivation of atmosphere!

They had the same focus, intention and heart. To build a revival culture it takes impenetrable unity and laser focus on a constant basis. With multiple services this makes it much more difficult. I am not saying that it cannot be done, but *I can confidently say that no two services will ever be the same.*

Unity in Leadership is Vital to Sustained Revival

Another crucial element of a revival culture is a church staff that is pushing together as ONE agreeing on things that matter to sustained revival. This fosters a unity which is absolutely vital to keep revival moving forward in the local church setting. Disunity is one

> Disunity is one of the primary enemies of revival and has been the decline and downfall of many of them.

of the primary enemies of revival and has been the decline and downfall of many of them.

Therefore, as senior leaders and as a church staff and as a congregation, we must be intentional about making sure that every area of ministry *owns* the vision of a revival culture. Whether it is youth, children, music, small groups, etc. they must view their ministry through the lens of revival...a sustained move of God. There can be no lone rangers using the church or revival to build their own name or platform.

Perfect unity releases anointing and this is what people sense as they come into your services.

To successfully cast this vision and have it stick, your staff and congregation must not only agree and participate in the revival culture, but they must pass this along to their leaders and workers as well. Every fiber of your church should breathe revival. We put a lot of *spiritual weight* on our people to *press, carry and contend for more of the Spirit* in their personal lives and in each service. We quickly realized that they must be equipped and prepared to cultivate the atmosphere *every time* they come to church. This weight absolutely *cannot* be cultivated nor carried by the pastors and staff alone; the people must bear the burden with you. We require the same level of pursuit of Holy Spirit of our volunteer leadership as we require of ourselves as a staff.

This is why it is imperative that you build a *spiritually mature* people who understand the press and the power of cultivating a free and open spiritual atmosphere in the corporate gatherings.

All that said, we must never forget that it all starts with the touch of the Holy Spirit on the hearts of the people. Without the touch of the Spirit you'll just have to keep producing things. Ultimately, people choose whether or not they will grow in the Spirit. We're talking about intentionally cultivating depth, building leaders and revivalists not just superficial, task-oriented people. I'm talking about building contenders not just attracting attenders. So, you will *never* be able to get away from the necessity of the wind of the Spirit consistently blowing on the hearts of the people, and as this is happening, your structure and building your people will be graced by the Holy Spirit.

The Mantle Clearly Defined

One Sunday after our morning service in June of 2016, the Lord orchestrated a divine meeting in our greeting room between me and a lady attending our church. She briefly came by and handed me a book that would prove to be confirmation and definition to our mantle of revival. As it happened, my husband and I were getting ready to go away for a few days to pray and fast into the revival. To this point we had been doing every Sunday night revival services since August of 2015.

The exposure of the revival was growing and we already felt that part of our assignment was to be a place where people and pastors could come and get an impartation of the fire of Pentecost and take it back to their cities and churches.

However, we didn't understand the magnitude of what was getting ready to be imparted to us as we began to read through the book. Every single chapter spoke not only to "who" we were and were supposed to be, but brought clarity and validation to *the identity* that we had already begun to walk in. With this God confirmation, we decided to change our revival meeting time to a once-a-month, four-service weekend (Friday-Sunday) and call it; "*Revival Weekend*", making it easier for pastors and other church attendees from other churches to attend and to receive impartation of a revival culture.

These weekends have grown tremendously over the last five years (at the writing of this book). I take you back to our 2013 declaration: "This Day we Fight for what we're Mantled to Be." That declaration (which is still in motion) set *off a supernatural causeway that would bring us into our full identity as a Revival Center in this Southwest Region*. If we can give God something to work with, He can move us into the greater that He has planned for us. Our mantle was revival. That day we made a decision to fight for it, to contend for more than the status-quo and nominal church and Christianity. I encourage you today, you may not be called to be a Revival Center, but you are called to contend for revival for your own life, family and your city. Fight for it! Every battle is worth it. The hunger grows and so does the resolve to be a doorkeeper of revival.

As we moved forward into years three and four of revival we reached a place where we needed to expand our sanctuary because we were at capacity. Once again, we were just following bread crumbs of the Holy Spirit. We busted the back wall out of our sanctuary to increase its size and accommodate more people to be able to continue to have one service as long as possible. Your obvious question is, what will we do when we fill that up? What will our decision be then? Our answer: *God will give you another bread crumb to follow.* Whatever you have to do to keep the atmosphere of revival alive, that you must do!

Gear Church or River Church

To further strengthen the mentality of a revival culture I want to share something that our youth pastor, David Schlueter, brought forth: Is your Sunday service like a gear or water, he asked? A gear is predictable; it's always turning and going the same direction doing the same exact thing. But water, when poured, is always going to land in a different place. *The Spirit is a RIVER.* So are you doing your service just to get through the "list" or are you letting God's river flow in your service?

The argument against this has been: God *"can"* move in this timeframe and structure. Some claim; "He CAN move within 55 minutes, and to that I say, yes, He can, but the issue is not that He "can" move within a certain time but that He's not allowed. The system doesn't allow Him to freely move. It so programmed to meet our time restriction that we're really not concerned about cultivation of atmosphere, just execution of a plan, a series or a program. *That is a gear.* The mindset becomes; we have to move through this to be finished in 55 minutes and we don't have time to waste. *Yet, we say we give the Holy Spirit control all the while we are controlling the atmosphere.* Five minutes of an emotional pseudo-spiritual high at the end of a gear-structured service will not bring a transformed life. For the sake of those needing transformation can we please stop pretending that the Holy Spirit is in control?

Nowhere is this more evident than in the worship and the preaching. Our worship team has a list of songs but it doesn't mean it dictates what they sing or do. As lead pastors, we've not given our worship pastor a time limit. This is something that we can do because we highly trust her ability to flow and move in the spirit and set the proper atmosphere for the altars and the Word of God being preached. When you have the controlled, gear atmosphere, it stifles the prophetic and it stifles the move of the Holy Spirit. We're not saying to allow things and people to go unchecked or to allow the service to go awry, or to go long in time just to say you've been at church a certain length of time. But when you have done your birthing and contending in the upper room prayer then you're moving into another level or sphere where it's not drudgery where people are laboring through this flow. Everyone is engaged because you've taught them to participate and not spectate. When you get the glory in the atmosphere, someone can *preach* 55 minutes and it flies by...compared to the entire service being 55 minutes and it feeling like the longest service ever.

> When you get the glory in the atmosphere, someone can *preach* 55 minutes and it flies by...compared to the entire service being 55 minutes and it feeling like the longest service ever.

The travesty is that people sit in geared services every week due to a philosophy that a "move of the spirit" keeps people away from church. So through human ingenuity we're getting people to church, but are their lives transformed to the point of radical conversions, living lives of holiness, set apart for Kingdom purpose? Or are they just coming and doing their time? In-and-out has become what it's all about.

Too many Pentecostal, Spirit-filled churches have lost the *fire and* there is little desire or passion to pay the price to get the fire back. The most significant loss is: *the tangible presence of God.* Everything always comes back to; "people *must* have a touch from God!" If they get just one touch of the presence of God it will mark them, and they will not want to go back to a church without His presence!

As we approach the end times, we must work very hard to detox our people from entertainment-based ministry. When entertainment is what we have to do *to get* them, we will have to do the same *to keep* them. There are people coming into our church weekly who have been looking for a radical, spirit-filled church for long periods of time not believing this type of church even existed. We have parents telling us they were raised in Pentecost, but their kids have never experienced it because they couldn't find it out there. There are potentially thousands of people in cities that are sitting in status-quo churches thinking, "Is this is all there is?", "is this is what church has become?"

Current trends and church growth models for Pentecostal churches have some positive and helpful systems and ideas that can be employed and bring strength to your leadership and your infrastructure and cause no harm. However, the *philosophy* on the moving of the Holy Spirit and the baptism of the Holy Spirit found in most of these models is to "*x*" out the Holy Spirit and the priority of God moving in the altars in your services. This philosophy came into the Church at large over a decade ago and we felt (*in the spirit*) the "quenching" of the irreplaceable moving of the Holy Spirit. And because of this, for about six or seven years, it was a war and a struggle for us in the area of our identity until we decided to *FIGHT* for what we were mantled to be…*a doorkeeper of revival.*

Our desire is to contend until this principality of resistance is broken through on behalf of Pentecostal churches in our city, region and nation. This spirit of the enemy has come and "set down" on Pentecostal churches deceptively luring them into becoming *Pentecostal*

> This spirit of the enemy has come and "set down" on Pentecostal churches deceptively luring them into becoming *Pentecostal* in name and doctrine only but not in practice and experience.

in name and doctrine only but not in practice and experience.

What I see as a by-product is that compromise has replaced conviction. Specifically in the areas of drinking alcohol, social engagement, a false message of hyper-grace all of which has dampened the fear of the Lord in people and could very possibly be sending some to hell. I realize this may be a *rant* to some, but to those who have ears to hear it will become *revelation*. When will we come to the end of ourselves and realize people need an undeniable touch of God? We must be real about this issue. If at the core of this philosophy is the limitation or the elimination of the Holy Spirit, this is a real problem that absolutely affects every other area. This is where the rubber meets the road…do we want good, polished, gadgets and gears or do we want *GLORY?!*

Our years of extreme warfare were beginning to make a bit more sense now on our journey. We realized that the pain of past seasons was more about "now" than it was that season. As I mentioned earlier in this book, we had repeatedly faced demonic warfare sometimes to the extent that we wanted to give up. The spirit of Jezebel was a primary foe and we were a *favorite target,* it seemed. As we moved into 2017, we realized about halfway through the year that this was our "year of authority".

Chapter Eight
Year of Authority

*N*ew levels, new devils is a familiar but very accurate statement. It is my belief and experience that many do not sustain revival due to the continued barrage of demonic attacks against a revival culture. The goal of revival is the sustained presence and power of God that results in transformation. This presence and power that we're contending for isn't nominal, it is fullness, all that God has and nothing less. The devil will let you remain nominal but begin to reach for fullness and he'll send out the troops and Jezebel is usually leading them.

Jezebel Hates Revival

Jezebel hates revival. Many have suffered defeat at the hands of this wicked spirit. The Welsh Revival which heavily influenced the Azusa Street Revival was brought to a halt by the spirit of Jezebel. This wicked principality hates the prophetic voice, miracles and any manifestations of revival. It is an anti-Christ, anti-anointing spirit that devises division and deceives sincere people who are seeking after the more of God.

"…I have *this* against you, that you *tolerate the woman Jezebel* (Revelation 2:19 NASB). *That which you tolerate will eventually dominate you* and this is what we saw repeatedly over our years as pastors pressing into revival. It seemed we would gain three steps forward only to be knocked back four or five. It became clearer than ever before that this wicked spirit was out to not only stop our ministry but to stop revival. What we couldn't see in the early days was ever more obvious in the year of 2017 - what I call "*The year of authority.*"

> It's all about the authority because the one with authority is the one with control, and with the devil, it's all about control.

You see, it's all about the authority because the one with authority is the one with control, and with the devil, it's all about control. Before Jezebel was a woman in the Bible, it was and is an ancient demonic prince seeking to overthrow God's authority. This spirit is evident in Satan himself who was the original usurper in heaven, trying to get authority that wasn't rightfully his. It didn't work with God, so he's been trying ever since to steal godly authority and he starts with you and me.

Jezebel is a demonic spirit, specifically a celestial power with worldwide influence that works in conjunction with the ruling principality over a specific territory. It influences territories, regions and nations, and of course, the people within. They issue assignments of evil in the earth which are carried out by demonic spirits (earthbound). Principalities are administrators of evil – the bosses under Satan – and they cannot be cast out they must be displaced. The more that you study this, the more you realize that most all, if not every operation of evil in our world, emanates from this spirit – Jezebel.

The Lost Spiritual Element of Contending

A church of revival must be a contending church. There must be a high level of spiritual intensity. A contending church eventually moves into heavenly governing and legislation which embraces the God-given authority to take dominion in the city, region and nation in which you have influence. This is where principalities and ranks of the devil are awakened and alerted to you like never before. You begin to impede on their territory using a greater power and an authority from God that is a blatant threat to them.

Many times, pastors and believers are not aware that their cry for more of God comes with more warfare. Their cry for more awakens a principality they've not met before. The devil doesn't come announcing himself. It will be in ways or through people we never dreamed, but he will weave his way into your minds, lives and churches for one purpose...*he wants your authority!* It is said that the devil comes to steal and the only reason you steal something is because you don't have it. The progression is to steal your authority in order to kill your spiritual reputation in order to destroy your spiritual influence. Influence is control, and remember, he's after control in the earth.

Spiritual authority is the right to use God's power to enforce spiritual law or the Word of God. It is a powerful weapon and the devil craves that kind of power and influence.

His authority was stripped from him by Jesus Christ so his only hope is to keep us from realizing the weapon of spiritual authority that we possess in Jesus Christ.

Our authority in Christ Jesus is the right to exercise His power in the earth and come against demonic forces. When we come into aggressive agreement with the Word and will of God, it releases a tangible assault against the devil and his schemes. However, if Satan can get you to *compromise your authority*, he can manipulate your life and church, your ministry and your mantle because it's all about the authority. His end game is to gain as much control as he can in the earth through deception, seduction and manipulation in order to control lives, governments, churches and secure territories.

> Behold, I give you the authority to tread on serpents, scorpions and over all the power of the enemy, and nothing shall by any means hurt you.
> Luke 10:19

Just like Daniel, there comes a point in your praying and your revival pursuit where you cross *a threshold of authority* that threatens the demonic and awakens a principality. However, at the same time, that same praying and revival pursuit releases angelic assistance and armies who begin to move according to the Word of God that your authority is decreeing in the earthly realm. Our prayers, like Daniel's, release archangels and begin to invade, dismantle and displace enemy-held territory. It launches spiritual arrows accurately to where a principality over a territory is moved and portals of heaven are opened and glory and the Holy Spirit is released over that territory making it easier for souls to come to Jesus. It breaks strongholds from cities. It frees regions and nations to hear the gospel and respond.

So, if I were the devil, I would do everything I could to rob people of their understanding of spiritual authority, keep them from realizing who they are in Christ because where there is no revelation of spiritual authority there will be no territory taken. Where there is no territory taken, the principality stays in place and in control.

What You Tolerate Will Dominate

In our early years of pursuit, before we officially began our turn into revival, we didn't understand what we were wrestling against. This was mostly our fault due to a lack of understanding and knowledge. I am aggressively opposed to those who withhold teaching from people about their spiritual authority and about demonic warfare. I do not believe that it should be our only message, but I do believe it cannot be ignored. Victory and open heavens over cities are directly connected to our understanding of spiritual authority and dominion and also to sustaining revival.

> Victory and open heavens over cities are directly connected to our understanding of spiritual authority and dominion and also to sustaining revival.

We fought for years, the unrelenting personal, mental, emotional and corporate attacks which manifested most of the time in personal pain or church division. As stated earlier in our story, we were at the end of our pastoral rope. But here in this chapter I'd like to say it this way, *we were at a crucial threshold.* Yes, it was a demonic attack, but it was also another chance to step up in our authority and cross that threshold into *a greater capacity for tenacity.* With every threshold crossing it may seem as if hell is on your heels, but what we have learned is that there's an entirely new army of angels that outnumber the demonic ranks that are waiting on your threshold crossover. They are there to annihilate the demons behind you and release God's purpose into your life, church and region. The Bible clearly tells us that we've been raised with Christ. The Bible also tells us that the devil is fallen. So if we're raised, and he is fallen, who has the upper hand in this war?

Like myself, most readers know the answer to that question, however, there is such a barrage of warfare as a revivalist that you must come to an undeniable revelation that you have complete authority over every attack of Jezebel. Don't tolerate it. Don't negotiate with it. Don't give it a platform or a voice. Throw it down! Because what you tolerate will dominate. Specifically, the spirit of Jezebel wants to silence the prophetic, weaken the apostolic and seduce the kingly authority. The prophetic voice is what dismantles it, the apostolic overrules it and the kingly authority is what ultimately kills it. If Jezebel can take out that three-fold function in your life or your church, the keys of authority have been kidnapped and that spirit has control.

I Found the Keys

I close this chapter with a personal story about spiritual authority. On Sunday, June 11, 2017 I had an undeniable prophetic sign given to me as we were at a very strategic threshold crossing in sustained revival. As early as 2014, I had lost a set of keys that opened every door to every building on our property at our church. I remember thinking that it was just odd that I had misplaced them. In other words, I could recall no reason that I should have lost them.

It seemed inordinate, not like any other random time that you lose keys. I looked everywhere for them and never found them.

On Sunday, June 11, 2017 I wore a pair of shoes to church that day that I had not worn in quite some time. The shoebox was toward the back of the closet. I grabbed the shoes from the box, put them on and went off to church. Let me remind you, we were at a strategic threshold crossing in our journey of sustained revival. The warfare with Jezebel had been brutal. We were learning and growing, but still had not come into full understanding of our spiritual authority in Christ.

The warfare with Jezebel had been brutal. We were learning and growing, but still had not come into full understanding of our spiritual authority in Christ.

The number 11 has been described as the *number of transition*. To cross a threshold, you must make a transition. The children of Israel were brought out of bondage in Egypt and the Bible says it was an 11-day journey to the Promised Land, or across the threshold. This means that on day 12 they would have crossed over. The number 12 represents *governmental authority*.

The particular day of this prophetic sign was June 11, or we could say, transition day. Day 12 was next, and if we crossed, it would take us into greater *governmental authority*. Between days 11 and 12, the children of Israel came to a place called Kadesh, or *a threshold*. There were decisions that had to be made at this place of transition. Spies were sent out to check out "day 12". Ten of them were intimidated and voiced their fear, two of them were mantled and ready to walk into greater authority and they too voiced their faith. Unfortunately, ten voices of fear sent one million people into 40 years of desert wandering because they didn't understand *their authority*.

That morning at church, my husband preached a message and part of it dealt with our spiritual authority. During the message he used his voice to speak against and serve notice to the principality Jezebel that had repeatedly attacked us. I believe this authoritative decree opened up something in the spirit realm over our church and over me personally. When we arrived home, I took off my shoes to place them back in the shoebox and as I look down, there in the box were the set of keys that I had lost years earlier! I did not see them that morning and there is really no reason that I should not have missed them. I believe the Lord hid them until after the service, after the declaration, after the crossing over of the threshold. I knew it was a prophetic sign and that God was showing me something spiritual with a natural event. I thought to myself, "I got the keys back"!

You've Got the Keys, Use Them and Don't Lose Them

I believe the Lord showed me the keys of spiritual authority in the spirit for our church and for revival and that they had been kidnapped by the enemy, specifically the principality of Jezebel. While we had attained a measure of spiritual authority, something was blocking the forward progression because some things were still under the control of this spirit. It needed to be confronted apostolically because it was trying to silence the prophetic and both are needed for a strong foundation of a revival church.

I fully believe at this point in the realm of spiritual warfare, the spiritual keys had been kidnapped. However, when confronted apostolically, it broke the control and the Lord used the natural set of lost keys, hidden in a shoebox for as many as three years, to show me, *YOU'VE GOT THE KEYS BACK, NOW USE THEM AND DON'T LOSE THEM AGAIN!* The inference of this statement meant that I had lost the keys at some point. I can't explain it except, many times we lose our keys of authority due to the fear of man. Sometimes it can be a process to get us to recognize this, but this day it was in plain sight!

You cannot forget the crucial part that the keys were in a shoebox. I felt the Lord say, "I put them in the shoes to let you know that where you walk you carry My authority and I will give you that territory!" God wants to grant us more authority. There are levels; even the demons recognize levels of authority. What I often say in the context of sustaining revival and raising revivalists is you'd better know your level of spiritual authority because the devil does. "Jesus I know, Paul I know, but who are you?"

The principality of Jezebel craves authority and will do anything possible to gain it illegally. This demonic entity understands that territories hang in the balance on the pivot of authority. It was at the threshold in the year 2017 that we stood with years of warfare behind us and yet the Lord graciously showed us that, *we had HIS KEYS of authority.* What we had lost through the fear of man, we had gained again

> What we had lost through the fear of man, we had gained again through our spiritual pursuit, unrelenting prayer and priority on the presence of God.

through our spiritual pursuit, unrelenting prayer and priority on the presence of God.

It was after this point that God began to lead our church into a greater influence over the nation and even the nations. But it all started with the decision at the transition point into governmental authority. Day 11 will take you into day 12, keep walking!

If you are to sustain revival, you must grow in your spiritual authority. Spiritual authority is best perceived and not explained. It's very difficult to put into words, but the way to obtain it is not a secret. The way to greater spiritual authority is the Secret Place. Much authority is given in the Place called Secret. God is the One with the authority, but the transfer happens only in one place, the Secret Place. To be much for God, you must be much *with* God. Revival demands a constant growth in authority, which demands a constant crossing of thresholds which demands a greater denying of flesh. I know it doesn't sound easy, and I promise you, it is not. This is not to discourage you; this is to prepare you. But if you are prepared, you will take territory, in Jesus name. You've got the KEYS! Use them!

Chapter Nine
Year of the Release of the Sound
We Won't Settle

*E*very element of revival is crucial to sustaining it. The *sound of revival* is included in a revival culture and it must be understood in order to cultivate. Revival has a sound and much of it has to do with intercession and worship. The sound of the God's Church in the earth releases His sound from Heaven and nowhere is this more evident than Acts chapter 2. The audible releases the inaudible. The natural releases the supernatural.

> The audible releases the inaudible! The natural releases the supernatural!

Worship and Prayer – The Power Twins

As revival continued into 2018, we began to place more and more emphasis on worship, specifically prophetic worship. It was very evident that prayer needed worship and worship needed prayer, which creates that "Twins of Power" against the forces of darkness. Together they *create a supernatural release needed for revival to be sustained.* In a revival culture, the value of His Presence is first and understanding the cost in cultivating it is essential in building and sustaining a revival.

Revival worship is instrumental in the cultivation of an open atmosphere. Beyond the obvious need for large amounts of prayer and fasting, you should strive to surround yourself with pure, prophetic worship leaders who produce pure, prophetic worshippers. This is something that we pray over on a continual basis. Once you have those people who have been cultivated with this mindset, you will have something powerful to release every time you come together.

In revival worship there is, and will always be, a level of contending, cultivating and then carrying it out. A very, very important element is *contending.* If you want an open atmosphere in your services you must be willing to contend, every time you come together. As a revival worship team, you are Judah and go before the others in order to shift and open the atmosphere for the glory. We don't fight *for* His presence; we fight to break barriers erected by the enemy that keep us *from* His presence.

Obviously, the enemy never wants us to do that and for this reason there will always be a contending in our prayer and

> We don't fight *for* His presence; we fight to break barriers erected by the enemy that keep us *from* His presence.

worship in order to press past the barriers of religion, flesh and the demonic. The Holy Spirit uses prophetic worship and intercession to accomplish this, and the more you press into this, the more it creates a *sound*. Once again, the audible releases the inaudible, the natural releases the supernatural. This leads to a very important factor in the area of music; the type of songs you sing in a revival culture is as important as singing them. You must be intentional about *what* you sing and even *when* you sing it. The *flow* in a revival culture is crucial. You do not have the luxury of *just going through a set* or singing the most popular song, even if it's good. If the song or set doesn't feed the revival atmosphere, if it doesn't open the heavens over the house and shake the gates of hell then it shouldn't be sung.

You also must leave room for the *prophetic flow*. You have to step back for a minute or even longer, listen to Holy

Spirit and make sure you have the direction to where He wants to go. Your prayer should be; *"Holy Spirit let us not ever try to go before you, or interrupt you, but let us be behind you, following You and able to hear you loudly and clearly."*

Intensity, Passion, Fervor, Aggression and Zeal

These words all describe the worshipper's heart posture in a revival church culture and it *never* lets up. Revival worship *always* has a *level of high intensity* and *spiritual confrontation* that is needed. This is found in your spiritual passion, pursuit and hunger. As leaders, the assignment is to provoke people to a new level of spiritual hunger every time we gather. Foundationally, revival will always go back to hunger, pursuit, and desperation for God and this plays out most in our worship and intercession. When you've tasted and seen, you know there's more so you must continually *push* to that level and intensity. You've got to push so as not to settle for average and nominal. There must be a constant pursuit to get to *the more. Never settle.*

The resolve not to settle in our personal walk with God and in our corporate church services is met many times with great opposition by demonic forces. This is very important to understand as you establish a revival culture in your life and church. So many give up and settle when the push back of the enemy begins to bring uncomfortable warfare and this is why so many settle for nominal to the sacrifice of revival.

As I mentioned in an earlier chapter, the declaration "we won't settle" has become our war cry and our heart cry. It speaks to both the Kingdom of Light and the kingdom of darkness triggering an alarm in both that a raw cry is lifted high from the earth that will not relent until we see His glory!

> So many give up and settle when the push back of the enemy begins to bring uncomfortable warfare and this is why so many settle for nominal to the sacrifice of revival.

This is why leading worship in revival requires that there is a constant challenge to the congregation to be a participator and not a spectator. There will always be a pushing against the *status-quo* and not allowing *complacency or slumbering*. You will get out of it what you put into it. We challenge the people to force their bodies to come into agreement with what their spirit already knows and to force their minds and bodies to align with what the revival atmosphere is demanding at that moment in order to release the more of God. In a revival culture, people cannot be

given the choice to *"let the team sing*

> In a revival culture, people cannot be given the choice to *"let the team sing to them and for them."*

to them and for them." A revival worship team needs to embrace these spiritual pursuit dynamics, they are non-negotiable.

Building a Revival Worship Team to Release a Revival Sound

With that said, you cannot staff a revival worship team like any other worship team. There comes a time in your pursuit of revival when you can't just give people a place to *"use their talent."* Unless they possess a pure prophetic, energetic and obedient heart in spiritual pursuit while leading worship, it will end up being a distraction and a dead weight.

The worship leader must have visible evidence that they have cultivated the revival sound in their secret place. This isn't something that can be copied from a popular recording music band, it must be cultivated in their personal secret place. This principle will also change the entire way that you build your worship team. At this point of revival worship, your team isn't just for people in your church that have musical abilities. When you go to this level, you must have people that are beyond just wanting to display and "use" their musical abilities, you must have talented people who carry great spiritual authority and understand Davidic worship.

This totally breaks the paradigm of how music ministry is usually done in a local church, but if you desire to keep a revival atmosphere you must transition beyond the usual into the prophetic. If people are not comfortable with this flow, the weight of it will crush and intimidate them. Having various people that you can rely on in this capacity helps fuel a revival atmosphere and back the worship leader in skill and spirit. It is impossible to sustain a revival culture without this very crucial element.

While possessing great personal spiritual passion, it is also crucial they also have skill. Much has been said about the necessity of both, however, in the context of revival, we want the "package" of the sound to be excellent to lend "credibility" to the revival sound. David played with heart and skill; we should do no less, especially in a revival culture. You also cannot underestimate the importance of building a culture of passionate, Davidic-type worshippers who are in a zealous pursuit of God that will create and carry this atmosphere every time you gather.

Prophetic worship must be given time. You have to completely give yourself and your service to it as a pastor, worship pastor and congregation. You can never rely on self, talent or your "list" and you cannot worry about time. You must give Holy Spirit the lead and let Him take control. To achieve this, you must have a capable people who has birthed the prophetic in their own life and also possesses skill.

As a lead pastor you have to allow and make the space for what needs to happen at that moment in the worship service. It is crucial that trust is built between the worship leader and lead pastor in this area because when that trust is present there is an unspoken freedom for both that helps to facilitate the free flow of the Holy Spirit. By no means am I advocating that the worship leader run the service, set the agenda over the pastor, but as trust is built and a true revival worship leader is at the helm, they will lead the people into a greater encounter with the Holy Spirit and at the same time set the atmosphere for miracles and the message.

The key here is that you do *not* allow the atmosphere to dictate you, you dictate the atmosphere. We *never* allow a dead atmosphere. We *challenge it* every time.

The key here is that you do *not* allow the atmosphere to dictate you, you dictate the atmosphere. We *never* allow a dead atmosphere.

We *challenge it* every time. When you challenge a dead or dry atmosphere you are challenging demons and flesh. One way that we do this is to *jump on it* in pre-service intercession. We engage in aggressive, intense, heartfelt intercession that *opens* the atmosphere as people are walking into our service. So many, if not most churches, are not taking advantage of their pre-service activity and are using it to make people feel comfortable, creating an atmosphere of comfort and ease and even using worldly music, light-hearted announcements, humor, media overload about non-essentials and all of this before the service begins. Then, they expect people to immediately enter into a high praise and deep worship. How?! Their minds have just been inundated with worldly, fleshly, funny non-essentials! We are The Church. We don't need to set a worldly atmosphere we should be setting a holy atmosphere! People do not need to feel the world when they come into the Church they need to feel heaven! *A spiritual atmosphere must be cultivated to encounter a spiritual God.*

Our pre-service intercession sets the bar. They break through barriers! The worship team then takes that bar and raises it continuously throughout the service. But the pre-service intercession is the first thing people hear when they enter our building and they know right off that we don' play when we come to church. They know it's not about "us" it's about Him. We hold strategic training for these intercessors and they have key prayer points that they hit every single service for the purpose of opening the atmosphere. This creates an audible sound that releases the inaudible sound of the Throne Room. The natural that releases the supernatural.

Prophetic Transition

To further enhance the flow of your service, it is wise to make good use of the time between worship and the preaching of the Word. One of the things that we have developed is what we call a *"transitional prophetic flow"* following the worship time and leading into the remainder of the service. A capable person who understands prophetic worship and flow should lead this portion of the service, preferably the pastor or staff member.

Worship shouldn't stop at the last song, it should build. At that point this person can effectively follow the prompting of Holy Spirit as to the need for altar ministry, worship, operation of the gifts of the Spirit, etc., that need releasing. This is a valuable time that is usually *wasted* in most church services but can be a great time and space for Holy

Spirit ministry as you gradually transition out of the worship experience into the next part of the service and the preaching of the Word.

When all you have is a block of songs that feels like a performance or a concert, you will not feel the need to have this transition because many times there hasn't been a real engagement of worship by the congregation and possibly even the worship leaders. When worship is done correctly, it is not a performance or concert but a journey to the Throne Room.

> When worship is done correctly, it is not a performance or concert but a journey to the Throne Room.

At this point, we shouldn't jerk people out of this atmosphere but strategically and prophetically lead them out and allow Holy Spirit to speak and move at that moment. If cultivated, this moment in your service can be powerful in ministry to the people as well as prophetic confirmation to the Word that is getting ready to be released.

Intentional Flow Sets the Atmosphere for Revival

Another important point to address along these lines is a common practice that has evolved in the church; the practice of timed-driven agendas that keep people from entering fully into the presence of the Lord. *An example is*: the worship leader comes out, greets the congregation and the team sings a couple of songs. At this point, the worship team backs away and another person comes to the podium to greet the guests for that service, after that another person comes to the podium to give announcements and take the offering. The worship team then comes back to the platform to do possibly a couple of more (usually slower) songs before the message.

Quite frankly, I am shocked that no one can see the detriment this is doing to the flow of worship and the atmosphere! This format does not give your people a chance to fully engage in the presence of the Lord. It is literally jerking them in and out of the courts of God, by interrupting their thoughts and bombarding them with all sorts of other stuff non-related to worship but yet expect a free atmosphere. Worship has a protocol clearly set forth in the Word. It is a journey from flesh to Spirit as seen in the Old Testament tabernacle.

But if we keep confusing people by standing them up, sitting them down, making them sing then not, then making them listen, or give, then try to worship again, we do not complete the journey and *our dead atmospheres reflect that reality.*

A priority that must be established for a revival culture is that *EVERYTHING* is built *around the moving of the Holy Spirit*. This may mean that you don't do announcements or even take an offering at the normal time slot. Who cares? If Holy Spirit is moving, that is all that matters. I understand we need the finances, but touched hearts usually means touched wallets and God honors when His presence is given honor.

Even after all of this, however, the worship team isn't finished with their assignment. They may be off of the platform but they are intently in tune with the Word preached and the atmosphere cultivated during the message to make the altar experience the best it can be. You can't just sing anything, it must match the Word. You don't want to quench what the preacher has cultivated. Even if you don't' have a song, this is where prophetic flow is a benefit. You can play chords and just sing in the spirit.

Worship leaders need to not to be fearful that a prophetic song will distract or shut people down. A prophetic flow demands a response from them and that they participate and lock in with the spirit. Many times a prophetic flow is easier for the people because it's fewer words. You have to step back and listen to the Spirit. You have to train your people in this, cultivate it. This moves them away from just singing a song. They're making a powerful prophetic declaration!

Sound alone is a powerful force. This earth was created by the sound of God's voice. I believe it is *being sustained by the sound of the voice of the Church.* To cultivate and carry the sound of the spirit on a sustained basis will be key to the end-time revival and outpouring in nations. Our God inhabits our worship, He rides on our sound and He arises with our shouts. We cannot allow this element to go unnoticed or uncultivated and expect a revival culture to be sustained.

The Holy Spirit will develop the unique and special "sound" of your house. It will correlate with the unique assignment of revival for your city and region. But there is one thing that must be realized, the sound of heaven is birthed from a posture that seeks for heaven's sound. Don't stop too short of what God wants to release through you. *Release the SOUND!*

Chapter Ten
Sustained Revivalists
A Mantle in Motion

*T*here comes a time when revival must produce revivalists. There must be a company of people as in the book of Acts who are committed to doing whatever it takes, for as long as it takes to keep the fire of revival burning on the altar of their hearts. A revivalist is a passionate believer who through Jesus Christ, revives, restores and redeems someone or an atmosphere that has died spiritually and leads them into a transformational experience with Christ.

I believe that as we move into the last days that sustained revival is as much a sign and a wonder as a physical miracle or strong deliverance. If the world can see the sincerity and longevity of a heart set ablaze with fire that once was dead, devastated and destroyed, they are seeing a sign and a wonder. Nothing is more powerful than a *product of revival.* The transformed life that revival produces is the greatest testimony of any revival. As we have navigated these years of sustained revival, we have been blessed to see salvations, deliverances, baptisms in the Holy Ghost and radical lifestyle changes. Many of these people serve faithfully in our church in various capacities and are a vibrant catalyst to the sustained atmosphere of revival.

Every believer is called to be a revivalist. The life and the ministry of Jesus and the early Acts church should continue through us today. In our day, we are writing Acts 29, the final chapter of the book of Acts, you and me, *revivalists of fire.*

"When the day of Pentecost had come, they were all together in one place. And suddenly there came from heaven a noise like a violent rushing wind, and it filled the whole house where they were sitting. And there appeared to them tongues as of fire distributing themselves, and they rested on each one of them. And they were all filled with the Holy Spirit and began to speak with other tongues, as the Spirit was giving them utterance." (Acts 2:1-4 NASB)

The Mantle of Fire

As the Spirit fell in the Upper Room it came upon the 120 as a *mantle of fire*. This was the *original* mantle straight from the wardrobe of heaven given to the early revivalists. It was a mantle of the *fire of the Holy Ghost*. God never intended for that we trade this mantle for a more popular, hipster, relevant, comfortable or easier one. The fire mantle was an intentional, pre-planned manifestation of God that He needed in this earth. Jesus passed that mantle to us through the promise of the Holy Spirit and he is asking today, *"Where are my revivalists of fire?"* Where are those who will wear the mantle of the fire of the Holy Ghost? Where are the preachers and intercessors of fire? Where are the marketplace and mission place ministers of fire? Where are those who praise with the fire?

The people in the city saw the *results of the fire* of the Holy Ghost on the 120 and asked, "what is this?" These mantled firebrands were *carriers of what their pursuit had produced.* They couldn't hide it nor did they want to hide it. Fire is very difficult to hide. *They were revivalists.* They brought restoration, redemption and revival to dead hearts and dead territories.

They were passionate and focused on the things of the Spirit. Passion and emotion of the Spirit are at an all-time low in the Church today. *There is little spirit of burning because there are no upper rooms.* It has become trendy to shut out the wind and the fire and *still* call it an upper room, yet the Word of God says; "Do not quench (put out; extinguish or subdue) the Spirit…" (1 Thessalonians 5:19)

I believe it is a strategic plot of the devil to have us *edit out* the fire because when the fire is gone the flesh is in charge. Holy Spirit fire is understood as the evidence inside someone to burn up what is wrong in their life and ignite what is righteous. Fire is the outward sign that something has changed on this inside. "He will baptize you with the Holy Spirit and with fire." (Luke 3:16 AMP)

Fire is recognizable. You cannot hide it. There is a burning that comes with the upper room encounter that cannot be denied. This burning becomes a continual yearning for true revivalists. They are dissatisfied to say the least and extremely frustrated at best when there is no fire of the upper room. They have learned the difference between *those who burn* and *those who merely bake.* The difference lies in the affect and the effect that it has on your life and the lives of others. A burning one will leave an indelible mark. A baking one is content with only a certain amount of heat in a controlled environment that is all about them.

Please understand, God *will not concede* to our ideals of lukewarm, comfortable Pentecost. He doesn't adapt to us; we adapt to Him. Don't forget that 380 people who saw Jesus after God raised Him from the dead missed out on the fire of Pentecost and therefore missed the mantle to burn! We're not told why they didn't show in the upper room that day, but as human nature goes, there could have been a myriad of excuses, unbelief and debate as to whether the command Jesus gave them was actually an acceptable and necessary thing to do. What are you missing out on today due to your negotiation with your flesh and modern interpretation of the Holy Ghost?

> What are you missing out on today due to your negotiation with your flesh and modern interpretation of the Holy Ghost?

Are You a Burning One or a Baking One?

You may have been baptized in the Holy Ghost but do you wear the mantle of fire and actually burn? Revivalists do! Revivalists *burn within* for more of God. They burn for His

Person and His purposes. Religion is offended by the heat of the fire of God on a "revivalist" so, don't be surprised when your burning offends someone who is not. *I give you permission to make others feel uncomfortable in their comfort.*

Fire is intimidating, in the natural as well as in the spiritual, it's just part of what fire does. May your fire increase the spiritual temperature around you so much that those with *altarless* lives and churches feel extremely uncomfortable.

In our first year of revival, I preached a series of messages called "We are Firebrands!" A firebrand is one who provokes, irritates and ignites. While we do not want to be arrogant about being irritating, we also do not apologize as a revivalist for making others feel uncomfortable in their comfort. Comfort is the breeding ground for continual, complacent spiritual compromise. Someone has to stir that up, and a firebrand or revivalist will do so.

Being a burning one isn't just a trendy phrase that supposedly identifies you with a revival group. It is a real passion that is imparted into your soul, the very fabric of who you are through a raw, real encounter with the fire of God and the God of fire. The spirit of burning is imparted

to you at your personal *fireplace* of the spirit. Your personal
upper room. You're set ablaze
as you gaze in His fiery eyes.
However, where there are no
altars (personal fireplaces) there
will be no inward fire.

You're set ablaze as you gaze in His fiery eyes. However, where there are no altars (personal fireplaces) there will be no inward fire.

Remember, sustained revival is keeping the fire burning
on the *altar and* that fire is recognizable. Imagine for a
moment that someone told you there was a fire next door to
you, yet when you went to look you see no fire. You're
frustrated and at the same time irritated that what you
thought was going to be fire turned out to be nothing. May
this not be the testimony of our lives and churches. We
advertise there is fire but when people come to look, it is all
a farce, no actual fire.

Sustained revival requires sustained altars. The fire
intensifies at an old fashioned altar of repentance,
consecration and pursuit. I am amazed at how many today
want *fun* when they come to church and are extremely
offended by the fire. *I choose fire over fun.* I can have fun at
the putt-putt mini golf, at the amusement park or at the pool,
but if you've ever tasted the fire of the Holy Ghost, fun falls
way short of anything that you want when you come to

church. Once you get a taste of the fire of the Holy Ghost nothing can replace it.

May we not be like the children of Israel who stood aloof at the foot of the mountain when God was burning in His fiery presence at the top. They were content to let only Moses approach. They saw it, thought about it, yet still chose to stay at a distance knowing that God was speaking and manifesting from the top of the mountain. *They were content to stay at the bottom making their golden calf while watching the fire of God burn.* This is a sobering thought. This is the same people who were led by the pillar of fire, the same substance as the fire on the mountain with Moses. They had once known the fire intimately. It guided them, protected them, provided insight for them yet now, they remained distant from the fire. *You cannot know the fire of God from a distance!*

The 120 in the upper room were infused with the same fire that Moses met on the mountain that day. *Upper room people run to the fire!* Many today are still in "Exodus", at a distance watching the fire and building idols. It's time to join the upper room and get *close enough to the fire* that *the fire gets in you.* Crush the calf in your life and burn for Jesus in

> You'll know that revival is being sustained when you see that the fire is sustained.

the city because this is what revival should truly produce. You'll know that revival is being sustained when you see that the fire is sustained.

Don't dare try to manufacture the fire, two priests in the Old Testament discovered that this is fatal. It will be fatal in your life, the life of your church and it will not bring glory to God. There is a pure mantle of fire waiting for revivalists who are desperate for more. You then become the revivalist who sustains the revival. This mantle is valuable and it must stay in motion!

"This Day we Fight for what we're Mantled to be!"

I remind you again of this vital declaration two years prior to the outbreak of revival. There was so much that tried to keep us from our mantle, yet it was this declaration that *set the intended mantle in motion*. The Spirit breathed on that declaration and we have been wearing the mantle ever since. The fight continues and yet resolve grows.

We were mantled for revival that produces REVIVALISTS! Doorkeepers of Revival! This seemingly simple declaration set in motion a desire to be a people and a place that hosts and cultivates a sustained move of the Holy Spirit and fire until Jesus comes back.

As you consider sustaining revival culture, please understand the value of the mantle. It comes with a resolve and an authority to accomplish everything the mantle requires and demands. Mantles come with different expressions each unique and custom fit for that person or place. Mantles are to be respected as they have been given by The Lord.

The devil wants you to compromise your mantle as it reminds him of what he gave up. He will attack you on many levels with the intent to cause you to dishonor and compromise your call and mantle. When this happens, you must always remember: *respect the mantle* enough that you *TRUST* in God who gave it to you and that He will break you through the tough times. The mantle represents a covering of divine affirmation that God has graced you for the assignment.

For us, the assignment was hosting, protecting, bearing the weight and responsibility of the mantle of revival on a sustained level. In a church culture that was rapidly embracing fun over fire, we had to consistently trust in God who gave us the mantle and do whatever it takes for as long as it takes to keep the fire burning on the altar and the door open to revival.

For our pastor friends please understand, *you may not ever have a MEGA church, but you do have a mega MANTLE…and that is enough!*

The Making of a Mantle

In 1 Kings 19:14, Elijah says, "*I alone am left…*" Jezebel had killed the prophets of God, Elijah had just left Mt. Carmel after calling down the fire of God to kill the prophets of Baal. I have typically viewed this statement by Elijah as a negative. I viewed it as though Elijah was copping out and God had to raise up three others in his place to accomplish the purposes He needed in the earth but I see it differently now. Elijah knew the value of a mantle and that he wasn't supposed to be alone, or the only one mantled. The prophets of God had been killed and he knew the mantle needed to stay in motion, so God said…to keep this mantle moving…start out with these three people.

"The Lord said – you shall anoint Hazael, Jehu and Elisha and if they escape one – the other will get them – there are 7000 "revivalists" who have not bowed to Baal. So he departed from there and found Elisha…Elijah passed over to him and threw his mantle on him. Elijah said to Elisha, Ask! What may I do for you, Elisha said, "Please let a double portion of your spirit be upon me." He took up the mantle of Elijah that had fallen from him…" (1 Kings 19)

Elisha's call gives us the expression *"take up the mantle"* which means to *pass an office or to operate in a function or anointing*. The cloak or the mantle represents the call as well as the transfer of authority and power to accomplish it. While the mantle itself was really nothing more than a coat in Elisha's day, what it represented brought a power and symbolism that equips the one who wore it with a *RESOLVE* to accomplish everything PLUS double the mantle demanded! Elisha did double the miracles of Elijah and this is the power of a mantle in motion! It is truly my desire that my children and grandchildren will produce double the revival results that I am able to accomplish in my lifetime. For this to happen, the mantle must stay in motion.

> It is truly my desire that my children and grandchildren will produce double the revival results that I am able to accomplish in my lifetime.

We have birthed a school of revival that is appropriately called "Mantled." At the writing of this book we are in our first class and within a year they will graduate, and some will be officially ordained. Sustained revival *must have* sustained revivalists.

When I look at revivals of past, I see a fervency of spirit and a laser focus of the spiritual eye of the shepherds and the sheep. I see a hunger to know more, see more and experience more of God. I see a passion for the lost that is driven by a personal encounter with the heart of Jesus Christ. When I look at revivals of past I see *a mantle in motion.* God visited a person or a people and the by-product was such *an explosive impartation* that could not be contained within one church or even one denomination, *the mantle required revivalists* that would surrender their all to the call and raise a distinct voice that cries "Where is the God of Elijah?!"

The mantle was then set in motion all over the world catapulting sons and daughters into ministry to the nations of the earth....*REVIVAL HAD BIRTHED REVIVALISTS!*

You could not contain them. They had to give away what had been given to them. History tells us that they would leave their homes and families to go to a country or land they had never spoken the language. They would set out on evangelistic campaigns in neighborhoods, cities, rural areas and regions to spread the gospel and the fire of the Holy Ghost! When you read history, you read what is possible and you also read about those who brought possibility into reality. This is what a revivalist does. He or she will take the fiery mantle and ignite revival wherever they go.

So, in our day, where are the revivalists that yearn to wear the mantle well? We are in a critical hour. I believe that Jesus is looking for revivalists of fire to stir and awaken saints and sinners alike. He is waiting to mantle them to strike the waters of revival again. He is calling for the voices of revivalists to come alive in this critical hour! May we be some of those who write the history of revival for this generation that future revivalists will read about. They will read about our passion, our resolve, and our determination to do whatever it takes, for as long as it takes to keep the fire burning on the altar and the door open to revival.

"That is why I would remind you to stir up (rekindle the embers of, fan the flame of, and keep burning) the [gracious] gift of God, [the inner fire] that is in you by means of the laying on of my hands…" (2 Tim 1:6 – AMP)

I hope that you will be provoked by dullness, by a life that is too tidy and too tame. I pray that your desire will be to have a heart that's inflamed, consumed with passion, moving with fervor and zeal. I pray that you will become a *revivalist who will keep the mantle in motion.*

Chapter Eleven
Well Diggers

*D*esperate people dig wells. This is true in the natural and the spiritual. Where there is thirst, there will be a desperate desire to dig for water. If you want revival, you must become a spiritual well digger. Every level of revival requires a fresh dig. So, for sustained revival, there will be a continual digging of spiritual wells. Our quest to find fresh water of the Holy Spirit never ends.

A natural well is freshly dug out and cultivated deep into the earth for the purpose of obtaining fresh water from an underground aquifer. An aquifer is a body of saturated rock through which the water can easily move. A well works only if there is an aquifer to feed it. Aquifers act as reservoirs for *fresh* groundwater. Groundwater held in the aquifer is one of the most important sources for water on earth. It is important to note how the well and aquifer work together to provide the refreshing fresh water supply.

Does Your Atmosphere Hold Water?

I see the well as our hearts, our spirit man who longs to be filled with the water of the Spirit. I see the fresh water as the refreshing presence of the Holy Spirit that comes with revival filling these *wells or hearts*. And I see the aquifers as the atmospheres through which this water of the Spirit flows. The water (Spirit) cannot fill the well (heart) successfully if it does not have an aquifer (atmosphere) to easily move through. Revival must have well-saturated aquifers or atmospheres to maintain and sustain the move of the Spirit. Remember, an aquifer allows the fresh water to move *through* it and then it supplies the well.

I have addressed our corporate atmospheres earlier in this writing, however, as I revisit this concept of spiritual well-digging, we must understand that the atmospheres *you* establish will either fuel and feed or starve and stifle the flow of the *water* of the Spirit. Yes, it is that important. Heaven

needs an atmosphere that

will welcome it. *You will not*

have a Holy Spirit takeover if

your atmosphere will not hold

water. Holy Spirit requires

an atmosphere or aquifer

that is conducive for *flow*,

or that He can easily *move through*.

> **You will not have a Holy Spirit takeover if your atmosphere will not hold water.** Holy Spirit requires an atmosphere or aquifer that is conducive for *flow*, or that He can easily *move through*.

This is a powerful revelation and one that is crucial to sustained revival. This concept can easily and should be applied to your personal atmospheres. Your personal atmospheres are just as crucial to sustaining the feed of the fresh water of the Spirit. There will come a moment in sustained revival where the individual must choose to grow with revival in this area. If they do not, revival will outgrow them. Unfortunately, we've seen this happen. Revival challenges the status quo and it challenges flesh. Personal atmospheres are many times justified and ignored until there is a revival challenge. At that point, the person must decide if they will cultivate the conducive *aquifer or atmosphere* around their life so that the Spirit has a place to flow in order to fill the well or their heart.

Cistern or Well? The Difference is Important

In the book of Jeremiah, the prophet tells the people that they have committed two evils; "…they have *forsaken* Me, the fountain of living waters, and *hewn* for themselves *cisterns,* broken cisterns, that *can hold no water.*" (Jeremiah 2:13 NKJV) We must be incredibly careful not to dig *cisterns in place of wells.* A cistern is defined as an *artificial* reservoir for *storing* water. When something is artificial it is manufactured by human ingenuity. It is a simulation or imitation. Just think what would happen if we spent as much time *digging fresh wells* of spiritual revival as we do *constructing artificial structures and systems* which are only cisterns and mere imitation.

> Just think what would happen if we spent as much time *digging fresh wells* of spiritual revival as we do *constructing artificial structures and systems* which are only cisterns and mere imitation.

A cistern does not require the hard work of digging, so of course we would rather settle for that instead of engaging in the difficult labor of spiritual well digging. However, it does not produce the same lasting, pure results as a well. A cistern is an imitation. Imitations are poorer quality and inferior. Cisterns are temporary, wells are permanent. Cisterns are shallow, wells go deep. Cisterns can only contain a limited amount of water and it is not moving water, it is stagnant water. We all know what happens to stagnant water, it attracts insects and fungus.

Wells contain fresh water, never stale. Our stale spiritual atmospheres are indicative that we have settled for a cistern. We have *cistern churches* that are being *mass-produced* because it's just easier and less painful to our flesh. Little spiritual capacity is needed to build a cistern church. However, there are many levels and dimensions of God that we can tap into. This means there are levels of revival also.

We serve a God of the limitless realms of glory. So many times, we think that we have tapped God out, we've reached His limit, when in reality *it is our limit* that we have reached. Yet He has realms of glory that we have never seen before just waiting, but it takes *a desperate heart* who's not afraid to get in the dirt and dig a little deeper.

> So many times, we think that we have tapped God out, we've reached His limit, when in reality *it is our limit that we have reached.*

The Bible says in Genesis that when the heavens and earth were created there was a mist that went up from the earth and watered the entire face of the ground. If you follow the "Law of First Mention" which is a principle that suggests that the first place in Scripture a word is found shows us the original intent of God, then this verse indicates that if we will dig, we will find water! In the natural, a large percentage of the worlds' fresh water is underground. Consequently, there is a huge resource of water lying hidden beneath the earth. Proverbs tells us that it is the glory of God to conceal a thing, but the glory of kings is to search it out, or I will say, dig it out. There are untapped dimensions of the spirit of God that He requires us to search or dig out with our hunger, desperation and spiritual pursuit.

The purpose of this is two-fold, *to reveal another aspect of His glory and to reveal another aspect of you.* He is pulling you into another level of spiritual capacity which will not emerge in a cistern mentality, it takes well-digging! Spiritual capacity must continually be challenged and stretched for sustained revival and for this to happen there must be a *sustained desperation.*

Desert Desperation

If there is one place in the natural which you get desperate for water, it is in the desert. We actually live in the desert of Phoenix, Arizona where it gets extremely dry and hot. Fortunately, many years ago there were *well-diggers* who wanted to see an extremely dry land well-watered. They looked at the land and they saw the vast potential for this territory. The only thing it needed was a consistent water supply to bring life and vitality to it. For this to happen, they had to get water to the desert. So, they starting digging because they were desperate for growth, life and potential.

Because I live in a natural desert, I understand a "desert desperation." We've all seen the old western movies of people stuck out in the desert, dry, hot, thirsty and desperate for water. This is fully accurate. However, in all of my years in this desert of Phoenix, Arizona, I have never once gone without water in the natural because someone years ago saw the vision of a very dry place well-watered and full of life so they just started...digging wells!

Your life, church or region may be very dry spiritually right now. It may look like there is no hope and no life. Yet, all it takes is one desperate person with a vision to start digging for spiritual water to be released. You then become that well and begin to create the aquifer or atmosphere that is conducive for the water of the Spirit to flow through.

Desert Discipline

I don't want to make it sound too easy, but I do want to make it sound reachable. Just like the desert I live in, most looked at it and said it was impossible for there to be life in this valley, yet today this area is over 4 million people strong and one of the fastest-growing counties in the United States. *It just took someone who wasn't afraid to risk, dig and keep digging until water reached the dry places.*

I want to impart to you today a desert desperation. Sustained revival must have sustained desperation, therefore, it must have well diggers. When you're desperate for God, you know He's always there, yet you want more of Him. There is a longing, a desperation that will not be denied.

> I want to impart to you today a desert desperation. Sustained revival must have sustained desperation, therefore, it must have well diggers.

David said, "O God, You are my God; early will I seek You; My soul thirsts for You; My flesh longs for You in a dry and thirsty land where there is no water." (Psalm 63:1 NKJV) A desperate person has great desire. When desire is depleted, spiritual dryness will creep in. In a dry climate, the ground gets hard and foliage becomes brittle. When the ground and fruit of your life or church are not continually watered with the Spirit, you produce dry atmospheres.

There are too many believers and churches existing in a desert while acting like they are well watered. However, the ground and the fruit are telling signs, my friends.

In our current church culture of comfort and prosperity; a me-centered faith and church structures that are geared to pleasing people, there is little room and even need for desperation. Spiritual dryness comes when we think we have enough. It doesn't come when we run out, but when we think we have enough.

When you stop digging, dryness sets in. When you think your cup is appropriately full

> Spiritual dryness comes when we think we have enough. It doesn't come when we run out, but when we think we have enough.

and you feel comfortable and safe, beware, soon you'll be a spiritual desert. A sustained desperation keeps us well watered in the Spirit. Revival requires holding a credible thirst and desperation. We teach our people that in order to have a sustained revival culture they must learn the *discipline of the desperate.*

To practice desperation consistently and intentionally is to remember what it was like in the desert region of your life or church do the things that desperation requires. If not, familiarity will set in, you will settle and your ground will be dry, your fruit brittle, you have left revival.

What has muffled your raw cry of desperation? What have you settled for? Have you stopped digging? Is your atmosphere confused and convoluted? Are you in a dry place? Is your fruit brittle? Start digging! Keep digging! Don't stop and revival won't stop. Consistently do the things that desperate people do and you'll reach water that will not stop flowing as long as you continue to be a well-digger.

"Therefore with joy you will draw water from the wells of salvation." (Isaiah 12:3 NKJV)

Chapter Twelve
The Persistent Remnant

*G*od is looking for those who will persist in revival. I use the word *persistent* because sustained revival, especially in the last days, will require this characteristic. It will be this spiritual quality that sets the remnant apart from nominal seekers and casual Christians.

We must understand that the closer we come to the end time; *Jesus is drawing the remnant line.* The devil is trying to dilute that line with deception and delusion when it comes to the cost and the cry for revival. Compromise will veil the hearts of those not willing to count the true cost of revival, yet want the fruit of it. The clear-cut distinction between the nominal church and the end-time remnant of the Lord Jesus Christ will be, persistence. Stamina, endurance, grit, tenacity, constancy and resolution will propel this remnant people

163

into great arenas of spiritual victory, as well as, spiritual warfare. Yet their persistence will keep them while experiencing both victory and warfare.

In the last days there will be a persistent remnant Church who will partner with the Holy Spirit to activate the Kingdom of God in the earth, release revival and the Lordship of Jesus Christ. They will enter strategic divine warfare with a victorious authority and tenacity while holding tenaciously to their love for Jesus Christ, the culture of revival and the gathered church.

This end-time chosen remnant will partner with the Holy Spirit's wisdom and clarity to expose deception and error while also revealing the heart of God for a lost and dying world. They will have postured themselves to continually hear the knock of the Lord at the door of their hearts and will consistently allow the Lord to deal with motives, ambitions, intentions and hidden areas. They will welcome the discomfort of exposure because they want a continual feast of intimacy and revelation of Jesus Christ.

This persistent remnant will endure slander and persecution and as revival grows for in the last day's antagonism against their personal lives and corporate gatherings will also grow. However, this opposition will serve to fuel a revival resolve and produce a revival harvest as well as a great endurance capacity.

"My fellow believers, when it seems as though you are facing nothing but difficulties see it as an invaluable opportunity to experience the greatest joy that you can! For you know that when your faith is tested it stirs up power within you to endure all things. And then as your endurance grows even stronger it will release perfection into every part of your being until there is nothing missing and nothing lacking." (James 1:2-4 TPT)

Through the spiritual keys of undeniable authority, the keys of heavenly worship and government granted by Jesus, doors of favor and influence will be opened as this remnant presses against the gates of hell and invades apathy and lukewarm atmospheres with a revival resolve.

This remnant authority will be used to expose truth and untruth, righteousness and unrighteousness, good and evil. They will operate in a purity of heart so that which is impure cannot stand. They will have a presence that cannot be ignored because of the spiritual authority that it carries. The persistent remnant will possess spiritual keys purchased with personal intimacy and cultivated through worship and communion with their Lord Jesus. Because of this, heaven's DNA will be transferred to them. They will echo the sounds of the Throne Room in the earth.

This persistent remnant may not be received by all, but make no mistake, they cannot be ignored. They will be the alarm of awakening, the rousing roar of revival and the voice that fills the void in the last days. They will not compromise, relent, bow or back down. They will persevere, press, plow and plunder the enemy's camp. They are forerunners, they go first and those that go first get hit the hardest so they can open the way for others to follow unhindered. This will be the persistent remnant.

> They are forerunners, they go first and those that go first get hit the hardest so they can open the way for others to follow unhindered. This will be the persistent remnant.

There will be such an uncommon anointing and an undeniable authority that it will intimidate religion and annihilate hell's deceptive protocol. Once again, not all will receive it, but none can ignore it.

The Plumb Line of Revival

This remnant will be doorkeepers of revival in regions and territories. They will hold the plumb line of revival in their region. "But these seven will be glad when they see the plumb line in the hand of Zerubbabel..." (Zechariah 4:10 NASB)

A plumb line is a visible marker showing what is *plumb or perfectly aligned*. There will be churches and revivalists in the last days who will hold the plumb line of revival in their hands.

People will look for and be drawn to those people and their locations. There will be an extraordinary hunger for the atmosphere that has been cultivated through the perseverance and revival resolve.

"When there is no clear prophetic vision people quickly wander astray. But when you follow the revelation of the word, heaven's bliss fills your soul." (Proverbs 29:18 TPT)

A plumb line can seem very boring, yet without it people wander astray and get out of alignment. There *will be* a remnant with a vision and a standard for sustained revival. Your region is asking for someone to show them, someone to lead them into a revival resolve. There have been many pure hearted people who tried revival. However, after meeting with increased warfare and the toll it takes physically, they backed off, gave up and settled.

The book of Revelation shows us seven churches and only two of those churches did not receive a rebuke from Jesus, Smyrna and Philadelphia. Both churches were warned of persecution, hostility, dislike and intentional attacks. It is clear from history that the church of Smyrna endured intense tribulation that came in many forms. *But during it all, both churches persisted in revival.* Symbolically, I believe these two churches represent the persistent remnant that will be in the earth in the last days. Persistent and perceptive, they will run the race with a raw cry for revival and they will see all things with eyes of the Spirit.

> Persistent and perceptive, they will run the race with a raw cry for revival and they will see all things with eyes of the Spirit.

A remnant is never the majority. It is a remnant or a piece or representation of something larger or bigger. There's the remnant and then there is the rest. And God's Word tells us that this remnant will be chosen.

"And that is but one example of what God is doing in this age of fulfillment, for God's grace empowers his chosen remnant." (Romans 11:5 TPT)

This remnant isn't exclusive but it will be selective. God is not an exclusive God, He prefers no one above another. This remnant is for whosoever will. The key word, however, is *will*. Will you choose to be chosen? Will you answer the call to be chosen"? It will not always be the popular choice or the current trend, but it will be the chosen remnant of God. Why is this such a big deal? Because the line of distinction between the remnant and the rest will be found at the crossing over into *chosen*. As soon as I step into chosen, I lose all identity with the unchosen.

"And they steadfastly persevered…" (Acts 2:42) A clarion distinction of the last days church will be that it mirrors the early church in all qualities and characteristics. The early church knew how to press and move under intense pressure. Revival will bring pressure in many ways. Like the early revivalists, we will learn to embrace opposition, warfare and persecution yet remain steadfast in our revival resolve. When revival comes it creates the atmosphere for radical transformation and radical opposition. The persistent remnant is equipped for both.

Why do I go to such length in this last chapter to speak about persistence and being part of the remnant? Because neither of these would be the first choice of the flesh without a sustained revival desire. There will be a constant pull backward into comfort and the crowd. This is where the *rest* dwell with absolutely zero resistance but also zero revival. If there is an overarching principle to sustained revival it would be, "I persist." No matter the pushback or feedback, I persist. There is a resolve that is birthed in you all the way back in that *year of pursuit* that cannot be compromised.

> If there is an overarching principle to sustained revival it would be, "I persist." No matter the pushback or feedback, I persist. There is a resolve that is birthed in you all the way back in that *year of pursuit* that cannot be compromised.

I encourage you and yes, challenge you right now, join the chosen persistent revival remnant. A region is waiting on your choice.

Epilogue
The Door is Waiting

O ver these years of sustained revival we have encountered countless people who've told us how hungry they are and how long they have searched for a church of revival. We have had people move from other states to Arizona for the sole purpose of planting their family in a revival church. When other pastors and leaders are searching for the next popular sermon series to run at just the right time of year, the people are yearning for a *fresh word of the Lord* carved out in the secret place of His presence.

These seekers long for pastors and leaders who have calloused knees and tear-stained floors. The craving in the heart of these people is for a church of substance and authenticity in the spirit. They are weary of entertainment and hunger for an encounter. They long for an atmosphere sensitive to the Spirit that releases the essence of the Throne Room. These hungry people yearn to see spiritual leaders who will stand boldly and cry loud and spare not; spiritual leaders who will sound the alarm for awakening in their cities and not just build an edifice to themselves.

On the other hand, there are desperate pastors and spiritual leaders who intensely desire a group of people who will contend along side of them for revival and awakening. These pastors are battle-weary, yet resolute in their desire for revival. They are looking for an army of hungry hearts who will be mantled as a revivalist for their regions. These pastors are tired of having to entertain, beg and plead for people to commit and even just come to church. They are weary of the Jezebel and the Absalom who've stolen peace and people from them. The longing of their heart is to fulfill the call of God on their lives and wear the mantle well. But they need hungry hearts to respond.

These two must find each other, the depleted parishioners and pastors. And when they do, revival is on. My hope is this book has ignited or reignited the fire, to find the door.

There are many doors that can be kept, but only the door of revival will bring the presence and power of God that result in transformation. It has been my observation that so many other doors are chosen while the one door that will unlock the DNA of heaven gets passed up. The door of revival is waiting for doorkeepers in all cities and regions so the presence and power of God can transform a nation.

I am a doorkeeper of revival. I pray you will be, too.

Made in the USA
Middletown, DE
11 January 2024

47680188R00099